RACISM, EDUCATION AND THE STATE:
THE RACIALISATION OF EDUCATION POLICY

Racism,
Education
and the State

Barry Troyna and
Jenny Williams

CROOM HELM
London • Sydney • Dover, New Hampshire

© 1986 B. Troyna and J. Williams
Croom Helm Ltd, Provident House, Burrell Row,
Beckenham, Kent BR3 1AT
Croom Helm Australia Pty Ltd, Suite 4, 6th Floor,
64-76 Kippax Street, Surry Hills, NSW 2010, Australia

British Library Cataloguing in Publication Data

Troyna, Barry
    Racism, education and the state: the racialisation
    of education policy.
    1. Discrimination in education – Government
    policy – Great Britain
    I. Title   II. Williams, Jenny
    370.19'342'0941   LC212.53.G7

    ISBN 0-7099-2498-4
    ISBN 0-7099-4316-4 Pbk

Croom Helm, 51 Washington Street, Dover,
New Hampshire 03820, USA

Library of Congress Cataloging in Publication Data

Troyna, Barry.
    Racism, education, and the state.

    Bibliography: p.
    Includes indexes.
    1. Education and state–Great Britain. 2. Racism–
Great Britain. 3. Discrimination in education–Great
Britain. 4. Intercultural education–Great Britain.
I. Williams, Jenny, 1938–   . II. Title.
LC93.G7T66   1986   379.41   85-22340
ISBN 0-7099-2498-4
ISBN 0-7099-4316-4 (pbk.)

Printed and bound in Great Britain by
Biddles Ltd, Guildford and King's Lynn

CONTENTS

For mum and dad (in Tottenham) and Gerry,
Jenny, Sophie and Toby (in Leeds) (BT)

For Geoff, without whom .... (JW)

ACKNOWLEDGEMENTS

We wrote this book during the academic year 1984-5 when Barry Troyna was Senior Research Fellow and Jenny Williams a Visiting Research Fellow at the Centre for Research in Ethnic Relations, Warwick University. Both of us worked in the Education team, which was led by Troyna, where along with our colleagues (Wendy Ball, Peter Foster and Krutika Tanna) we carried out research on antiracist education initiatives in various LEAs, schools and colleges. In the course of our research we have been helped, directly and indirectly, by many people. We would like to thank them all and hope that this book is, in some ways, a repayment for the co-operation and friendliness they have shown towards us. Amongst them we would like to thank, in particular, Gerry Davis, Andy Dorn, Dawn Gill, Bill Gulam, Peter Newsam, Barbara Plant and Robin Richardson for discussing antiracist education initiatives with us and for providing important and 'difficult-to-get-hold-of' documents which facilitated our understanding and analysis. Wendy Ball, Bruce Carrington and John Solomos also deserve our thanks for reading and commenting critically on an earlier draft of the entire text. As co-directors of the Centre, Robin Cohen and John Rex have supported our endeavours, for which we are grateful. Finally, and most importantly, we are indebted to Rose Goodwin and Gurbakhsh Hundal who translated draft after draft of illegible scripts into presentable form. We put excessive demands on their time, patience and characteristic good humour; despite this they have done a wonderful job for us.

The book was jointly conceived and jointly undertaken and it comprises an amalgamation of our theoretical and empirical concern with antiracist education over the last decade. However, a division of labour was necessary, on occasions, to expedite its completion. Barry Troyna drafted the original versions of chapters 1 and 2 and Jenny Williams wrote the first drafts of chapters 3, 5 and 6. Nonetheless, we are equally responsible for what follows.

BT (Sunderland Polytechnic)
JW (Wolverhampton Polytechnic)

INTRODUCTION

In 1982, Michael Parkinson suggested that social scientists in the UK had failed consistently to analyse, either in theoretical or empirical terms, the processes of decision-making and policy formation in the sphere of education. 'The most striking feature of the British literature in this field', Parkinson wrote, 'is how relatively little of it there is' (1982, p.114). Until very recently, his criticism was especially apposite when it came to studies of racial matters in education. Indeed, as Andrew Dorn and Barry Troyna pointed out not so long ago, the proliferating literature in this field reflected an almost obsessive commitment to micro-level analysis; that is, the bulk of the literature was concerned with classroom matters and was dominated by discussions about 'the issues of language, curriculum development, pupil-teacher interaction and comparative academic performance' (1982, p.175). Naturally such issues should constitute an important element in the literature; the point which Dorn and Troyna stressed was that such a narrow perspective did not, indeed could not, identify the political and policy framework in which these and related issues were located. They argued that a framework built along these reconstituted lines was essential if the issues and findings uncovered by micro-analyses were to form more than a series of disparate factual data.

It is difficult to do much more than speculate on the reasons for this uneven, decontextualised, even politically naive approach to racial issues in education. We suppose it may be partly due to the apparently traditional lack of interest in this mode of enquiry which Parkinson referred to. It may also have stemmed from the view that in the prolonged absence of explicit policy prescriptions for racial matters in education there was little of substance for social scientists to study and analyse. To some extent this is an understandable reason. After all, the Department of Education and Science (DES) continues to turn a blind eye to demands from within and beyond the education service for a clear, unequivocal policy commitment to multicultural or antiracist education (Tomlinson, 1981a; Troyna, 1982). Its only significant move on this issue came in the 1977 Green Paper, Education in Schools: A Consultative Document, where it asserted that: 'Our society is a multicultural, multiracial one and the

1

curriculum should reflect a sympathetic understanding of the different cultures and races (sic) that now make up our society' (1977, p.41). Hardly then a firm policy; even less an injunction for formal action by Local Education Authorities (LEAs), schools and their teaching staff. Similarly, it was not until the early 1980s that any significant number of LEAs considered the issues important enough to publish formal, Authority - wide policy statements affirming a commitment to multicultural/ethnic or antiracist education. In sum, before the 1980s the development of practices and procedures which integrated black perspectives into the educational process depended largely on the initiative of individual teachers, the campaigning efforts of groups such as the National Association for Multiracial Education (NAME) and All London Teachers Against Racism and Fascism (ALTARF) and the pressure exerted by various black parents, student and community collectives.

Against this background of apparent inertia it seems likely that social scientists considered analyses of decision-making and policy formulation processes, both at national and local government level, wholly inappropriate. Ironically, this view may have gained credence with the first major study of the UK's educational response to black students in its schools. There the author, David Kirp, argued that with one conspicuous exception (i.e. the dispersal or 'bussing' issue) there was and never had been a 'racially explicit' policy at national level (1979). The legitimacy or otherwise of Kirp's arguments is not at question here, we shall scrutinise them in the following chapter. The important point is that his analysis seemed to substantiate and endorse the claim that neither the DES or individual LEAs had explicit racial policies, and, therefore, there was little of substantive importance to analyse. The problem with this assumption is that it fails to recognise that inaction or consistent decisions not to act also imply the existence of a policy (Bachrach and Baratz, 1962; Lukes, 1974). Put another way, neither inaction or inexplicitness can be easily dismissed as featureless non-events; both constitute explicit ideological positions. In education, for instance, inaction and inexplicitness may be seen as positive responses to racially perceived situations, or so we shall argue. So far, however, this seems to have been discounted in analyses in favour of more behaviouristic definitions of 'policy' such as the one provided by Keith Fenwick and Peter McBride: '...when the term "policy" is used it is presumed to refer to consciously undertaken changes of direction and priority in relation to the services as a whole' (1981, p.31). Given the pre-eminence of this definition it becomes easier to understand why the study of race relations policy in education has become progressively more attractive to social scientists since the onset of the 1980s. Since then (and despite the DES continuing hesitancy and ambiguity in this area) race relations policy has acquired a much higher profile in the education service and over 30 LEAs now possess formal and explicit policy statements and documents. Put bluntly, their stance is more overt.

The causes and effects of this change, (i.e. the development of educational policies which focus explicitly upon the 'racial' nature of society), constitute the central problematic of this book. It is our contention that such an analysis needs to consider not only the changing public stances of central and local government but also the political and educational ideologies on which these public stances and policy positions have been predicated. There are many different ways in which this task could have been undertaken. Indeed in the past two or three years there have been a plethora of books and articles upon 'race' and education. In this introduction therefore we will outline our main conceptual and analytical tools and demonstrate the specific concerns of this project which differentiate it from other recent studies.

Our distinctive and initial orientation is to take as a focus the theme of 'racialisation'. Since the series of post-war UNESCO conferences on the 'race' question (held in 1947, 1951 and 1964) social scientists and biologists have generally agreed that the designation of the world's population into distinctive racial categories can no longer be considered a tenable scientific exercise. That is, whilst 'race' might have limited use as a taxonomic concept, the possibility of racial differences being biologically based has been generally rejected. Despite this, 'race' continues to be used in both popular and academic discourse, to mean, as Pierre Van den Berghe suggests, 'a group of people who are socially defined in a given society as belonging together because of physical markers such as skin pigmentation, hair texture, facial features, stature, and the like' (1984, p.217). Social scientists have been interested in both the reasons why people believe in the existence of 'races' and the ways in which their behaviour is affected by those beliefs. The term 'racialisation' refers to the complex processes through which racial designations have been established. As Robert Miles notes, it is:

A term which has emerged in analysis in the 1970s to refer to a political and ideological process by which particular populations are identified by direct or indirect reference to their real or imagined phenotypical characteristics in such a way as to suggest that the population can only be understood as a supposed biological unity (1984, p.223).

What has interested Miles has been an historical account of the economic, political and ideological conjunctures when this process has occurred (Miles 1982, 1984 for example). Along with others interested in this issue, Miles points to politicians, the media and the police as crucial agents through which such ideological developments occur (Miles 1984; Hall et al 1978; Joshua and Wallace 1984). We want to extend this and look at the role of education in these processes. In short, we want to establish how far assumptions and prescriptions contained in educational policy and discourse reflect and contribute to this racialisation process.

In order to explore this particular theme it is important to delve more deeply into what is meant by racialisation. As Miles indicates later in his piece racialisation is almost always a racist process, in that it is based upon an imposed hierarchical ordering of groups on the assumptive grounds that some groups are better or worse, superior or inferior.

Racist ideologies normally accompany racialisation even though the process no longer relies solely on the theories of scientific racism. As Martin Barker (1981) has indicated, scientific racism has been superceded by 'the new racism', a belief that certain groups of people, usually national groups, have distinctive, inherent and superior ways of life which are threatened by outsiders. In Britain in the past four decades these outsiders have been defined initially and primarily by their skin colour.

At this point the general reader and those involved in education might be alarmed at our suggestion that the educational system in the UK has played a prominent part in endorsing and perpetuating racialisation processes. We shall substantiate the claim in the following chapters, and in undertaking the empirical work necessary to do this we have found that certain analytical tools developed by Frank Reeves (1983) have aided our thinking. Like Miles, he is interested in racialisation, particularly in UK political debates, and in this context he uses the notions of discursive racialisation and deracialisation. Reeves makes the point that racial evaluations in political discourse may be overt or covert and geared towards either benign or racist goals. For example, he refers to 'discursive deracialisation' to typify a situation in which 'persons speak purposely to their audiences about racial matters, while avoiding the overt deployment of racial descriptions, evaluations and prescriptions' (1983, p.4). This covert use of racial evaluations serves important political purposes, writes Reeves, because it is often capable of 'justifying racial discrimination by providing other non-racist criteria for the differential treatment of a group distinguished by its racial characteristics' (1983, p.4). The U.K's immigration laws of 1962, 1965, 1968 and 1971 constitute classic exemplars of 'discoursive deracialisation'. All were geared, to a greater or lesser degree, to a racially selective mode of immigration control, though none was openly framed or rationalised in these terms. In most political discourse non-racist criteria (such as overcrowding, additional strain on scarce resources and so on) were invoked as justificatory conditions. In contrast, 'discursive racialisation' denotes the explicit use of racial categorisation and evaluation. This may be directed towards avowedly racist aims such as when it figures in theories of fascism or scientific racism. Conversely it may assume benign forms; when used in this latter sense discursive racialisation 'reflects a growing awareness of and indignation at racial injustice. Racial evaluation and prescription is directed at refuting racism and eliminating racialist practices' (Reeves, 1983, p.175). Support for ethnic monitoring from the Commission for Racial Equality (for example, CRE, 1984) and from various Local Authorities might be seen as examples where discursive racialisation is directed towards eliminating racialism via the identification of racial inequalities. This form of 'benign' racialisation summarises the focus of current antiracist education debates. Because these debates make explicit reference to perceived racial differences and centralise these in subsequent policies they could, in other contexts, be seen as racist. However, because they represent a genuine intention to minimise racial inequalities and discrimination by first identifying where these are present, such a characterisation would be inapproriate. In short the concepts of discoursive deracialisation and benign racialisation as defined here provide the means by which we can clarify and analyse the ways in which LEA ideological and policy responses on racial matters have developed in the U.K. since the early 1960's. They enable us to explore the muddled and contradictory ways in which 'race', ethnicity, culture, social class and deprivation have been presented and related. They also allow us to develop insights into the relationships between benign and racist forms of racialised discourse. Finally we can situate these discoursive developments in a broader context and consider their relationships to wider racialisation processes: to the economic and political contexts within which such ideological developments occur.

As we have stated the prime context of our study is the education system. We will therefore now outline briefly our understanding of the role of education in contemporary society. The relationship of education to changing capitalist economic and democratic states has figured largely in recent literature in educational sociology (see Dale, et al, 1981; Giroux, 1983 for useful summaries) and how and where one engages with this debate depends very much on the nature and focus of one's work. At the present time no sociological study of education can afford to ignore the ways in which the fiscal crisis and restructuring of industry in the U.K. are mediated by the state through various economic, political and social policies. This general process which includes policy changes in the spheres of housing, welfare, employment and unemployment and so on, affects local areas differentially and provides the setting in which educational problems are perceived and experienced. This study is concerned with education policies developed by LEAs and it seems to us that the relationship between these national (and international) developments and local policy responses is not direct and clear-cut. For this reason we do not endorse the neat, deterministic presentation of international and national developments presented by Chris Mullard (1984), in which LEA policies are directly related to the processes of decolonisation, neocolonialism and the deconstruction and reconstruction of capital. Rather we would see these world wide processes of change and the particular forms they assume in this country being mediated by the state. This determines the structural, political and ideological parameters within which local politicians and bureaucrats operate. But LEAs are also subject to other determinations and in this sense they may be said to constitute sites of struggle. This complex relationship between structural and ideological constraints, on the one hand, and local policy options, on the other, gives rise to the sociological term, relative autonomy. But, as Andy Hargreaves points out, it is difficult to give real meaning to this term except in the context of a detailed, empirical study:

> ... relationships between education, the state and capitalism cannot be explained at the level of theory alone but must be demonstrated through detailed treatment of empirical evidence. At some point or other, then, it is important that the speculations of theoreticians are squared with the "real world" (1983, p.27)

This, then, is our aim: to provide an empirical study of policy changes in LEAs which takes account of the economic and social processes of the central state and the consequent forms which local options assume. As we pointed out earlier, studies of education policy-making in general are few and far between. It follows that even fewer studies of this area exist within the theoretical framework in which we are working. Even so, the work of John Ahier and Michael Flude (1983), Henri Giroux (1983), Brian Salter and Ted Tapper (1981) and Geoff Whitty (1983) have, in different ways, provided guidance and inspiration. Let us look briefly at the ways in which they specify the educational contexts in which educational policy-making is set.

To start with, these writers agree that education does not create structural inequalities directly but that its prime concerns are cultural and ideological. It is through these processes and orientations that education reflects, reproduces and legitimates inequalities. It is precisely because of the education systems relative independence that it is able to win general consent for the differential treatment of and allocation of rewards to students that enables it to confirm inequalities generated elsewhere. For Giroux, and Salter and Tapper the functions and aims of the educational system are legitimated in one or more of the following ways: the economic needs of the society; the democratic needs of society and respect for individual development. The priorities assigned to these concerns are not static however; they are both periodic and related to particular age stages in the educational sector. What is more, the substantive policies which follow from or are legitimated by these key ideological concerns are subject to contestations, resistances and compromises. This enhances our view of LEAs as 'sites of struggle' but, once again, this is a term which can only be made meaningful and persuasive through empirically-based detail and insights. As Giroux informs us, in all social formations there is room for self-creation, mediation and resistance; consequently, 'there is a substantial difference between the existence of various structural and ideological modes of domination and their structural unfolding and effects' (1984, p.259).

Briefly, then, we see policy-making in LEAs as a product of local political conflict which is set within limits defined primarily by the state but also by established professional and bureaucratic hierarchies. At this level, ideological conflicts related to specific problems and their resolution, reflect the interests of particular groups whose strength depends partly upon the institutional context in which they operate and the resources they can command, partly also on the intellectual appeal of their programme. In order to appeal to a wide audience these ideologies must find resonance with other groups who are needed as allies. These potential allies must recognise enough common interests which will induce them to identify with and support key aims. At the same time, these interests and aims may be reinterpreted in such a way that they concur more closely with the potential allies' own definitions of problem situations and their own 'expert' ways of dealing with those. For example, teachers often reinterpret the educational problems of their students in terms of their own professional expertise in, say, language matters, remedial education and so on. But this reinterpretation and incorporation of ideologies is usually partial, rather than complete. Thus whilst (mainly white) teachers may accept that the ideology of racism constitutes the lens through which the experiences of black students in school might best be viewed, their perception and understanding of this ideology rarely corresponds precisely with the understandings of black parents and students. These black perspectives will have some influence on the shape and thrust of policies - if only because black students are often singled out as the 'objects' of policy - but it is unlikely that they will be fully represented and integrated in these policies. The ideological and political forms of resistance from groups who are the 'objects' of policies will be one important influence on the formation and implementation of those policies.

What we have said so far can be summarised like this: studies of policy-making in LEAs need to embrace two major concerns. They need to acknowledge the broad political, social and economic contexts in which policies are generated because these allow us to identify the constraints imposed on the nature and extent of educational change. They must also recognise the process of policy generation. These alert us to the ways in which the impact and consequences of broader issues and developments are mediated and redefined in the local arena by educational professionals, bureaucrats and local politicians, all of whom tend to operate with established ideological assumptions about the functions of education. This complex relationship between broad state forces and concerns and the specificity of local responses to these issues is what we mean when we use the terms, relative autonomy and sites of struggle. While we recognise the overall primacy of the state it is in the arena (or 'space') opened up by this relative independence of the local education system that the competing ideologies of different groups arise and are resolved, either partially or wholly.

One of the reasons we need to emphasise local variations and the relative power of local groups to influence outcomes is because this study is not concerned with educational ideologies originating from or initially sponsored by central government. Instead, our concern is with the periphery (LEAs) and the emergence and advocacy of ideologies in the periphery by what might be seen as 'subordinate groups'; that is, particular groups of teachers and black organisations and individuals. What happens to these demands once they are heard by educational policy-makers is an important theme in the book.

It should now be clear that we are concerned with the formulation rather than implementation of policy. Some writers prefer to see these as distinctly different processes, involving different people and predicated on different rationales. We would not want to make this distinction quite so clear-cut because it seems to us that a study of policy formulation is a prerequisite of an understanding of the problems of implementation (Troyna, 1985a). Policy rhetoric, nevertheless, does serve essentially ideological purposes and in the sphere of education what often emerges are what Michael Apple defines as 'slogan systems' (1975); that is, rhetoric aimed at changing the conventional patterns of interpretation. As our analysis develops it will be clear that we view antiracist education as a slogan system of reform, par excellence. It is an educational ideology which is sufficiently broad to encompass a variety of people who might have disparate opinons on other matters but who will willingly co-operate on this particular issue. As a multicultural education adviser put it to one of us: 'Multicultural education is like virtue, everybody's in favour of it'. At the same time, antiracist education, in line with other slogan systems, is specific enough to provide concrete suggestions for action which 'make sense' to different groups of people. The extent to which slogan systems generally, and antiracist education in particular - as expressed through policies - are internally consistent, educationally coherent and politically and ideologically viable is an empirical issue. We can only make judgements on these matters on the basis of a detailed scrutiny of policies and through interviews with 'key individuals' and these provide the empirical meat of our book. But on what political and ideological grounds do we make those judgements? It is almost a platitude to say that social science is neither objective or impartial. Indeed, as Thomas Popkewitz (1984), and others have noted, social sciences are socially constituted discourses. We are therefore influenced by contemporary social science theories, by our occupational culture as educational/social researchers and lecturers (and formerly, school teachers) and by our involvement in local antiracist politics. We recognise the pervasive and iniquitous existence of racial inequalities and discrimination and racist ideologies and work towards their mitigation. It is from these standpoints and commitments, therefore, that we are interrogating and evaluating the efficacy of LEA policies.

The plan of the book is to trace the political history of racial policies in education. In chapters 1 and 2 we focus on the rise of multicultural education as a paradigm of educational change in the 1960s and 70's, both in the national arena and in specific local contexts. We then turn our attention in chapters 3 and 4 to the emergence of an alternative mode of understanding which has been informed by theories of institutional racism. Then in chapters 5 and 6 we focus critically on why and in what ways this newer mode of understanding has been integrated into the formal policy statements of seven LEAs in the U.K. The conclusions take us back to the central theoretical and political questions of the book; namely in what economic and political contexts has the racialisation of educational policy taken place; what forms has it taken and what policy options do LEAs have, given a political commitment to mitigate racial inequalities and racist ideologies.

Chapter One

DISCRIMINATION BY PROXY: THE DERACIALISATION OF
NATIONAL EDUCATION POLICY AND DISCOURSE (1960-1980)

Before turning to LEA policies it is necessary to set the national
context of debates concerning 'racial' issues in education from 1960-
1980. In our introduction we drew attention to David Kirp's important
contribution to understandings of how policy-makers and others in the
UK education system, both nationally and locally, have perceived,
defined and responded to those issues conventionally designated as
'racial'. It would be misleading, however, for us to give the
impression that Kirp has been the only contributor to this debate. On
the contrary, the writings of Eric Bolton (1979), Hazel Carby (1982),
Chris Mullard (1982) and Barry Troyna (1982) have helped to enhance
an understanding of the way in which educational policy and ideology
has developed in this area since the 1960s. Their specification of
ideological and policy approaches in terms of assimilation through
integration to cultural pluralism provides a framework upon which our
analysis will build. The point we want to stress is that Kirp's analysis
has been largely unchallenged and has attracted considerable
attention and support on both sides of the Atlantic. It is now time to
take his analytical framework seriously and deconstruct its
ideological and political foundations.

'RACIAL INEXPLICITNESS' REVISITED:

Briefly put, Kirp argues that at least until 1981 these policies
could be conceived of in terms of their 'racial inexplicitness', a term
which comprises descriptive and evaluative dimensions. Firstly, he
argues that the term has descriptive power in that it allows a
distinction to be drawn between the ways educationists in the UK and
USA have engaged in policy formulation. In the USA, for instance,
'race' has figured prominently on the educational policy agenda at
least since 1954 when the Supreme Court ruled that segregated
schools were unconstitutional. As Kirp put it in his more recent book,
<u>Just Schools</u>, the central tenet of the Supreme Court's decision was
that 'individuals deserve to be treated as persons, not as members of a
caste or class' (1982, p.12). Since then, the divisiveness of racial
inequality has been an important focus of social policy intervention in

the USA where in Kirp's words 'racial fairness and educational equity' have been seen as 'tightly linked' (1982, pp.32-33).

In the UK, however, Kirp argues that 'race' did not figure openly as a basis for policy interventions; rather, race-related concerns were embedded in a range of 'racially inexplicit' educational categories. Kirp also imposes an evaluative dimension to the term when he writes: 'In the usual instance, inexplicitness implies doing nothing concerning race. The term may also mean doing good by stealth' (1979, p.2). And later in the book Kirp reaffirms what he sees as the benefits of this 'doing good by doing little' approach: '...one helps non whites by not favouring them explicitly. The benefits to minorities from such an approach are thought to be real if invisible - or better, real because invisible' (1979, p.61. Original emphasis). In the distinctive, almost idiosyncratic manner in which Kirp defines and operationalises the term, 'racial inexplicitness', it is both inappropriate and misleading. As such it should be discarded and replaced by more precise and analytical concepts. Now this is not simply a matter of semantics. Rather, it allows for a more accurate political account. This is because the concepts we shall use to analyse the development of educational policies on racial matters will convey more precisely the ways in which ideological and political imperatives determined which of the demands arising from the black communities and antiracist pressure groups were met by policy-makers and which of these demands were excluded routinely from the agenda. In short, they have a superior descriptive and explanatory power.

The concepts we want to use were referred to in the introduction and derive from Frank Reeves' study of British Racial Discourse (1983) They are (discoursive) deracialisation and (benign) racialisation.

From the definitions of these terms it should be clear why our reformulation of the 'racially inexplicit/explicit' designation of educational policies into the 'deracialised/racialised' categorization is of ideological and political significance. The educational policies which comprised race-related elements in the 1960s and '70s were unable to satisfy the demands of the black communities precisely because they were deracialised and did not engage with the issue of racism. Despite Kirp's claim that they did 'good by stealth' they did not, indeed could not, conceive the educational system as a site in which the reproduction of racism in Britain is confirmed and achieved. As such they failed to meet the most basic demands of the black communities and anti-racist groups: namely, that the perpetuation of racial inequality in the school needed to be undermined by forceful policies and practices.

The concept of deracialisation therefore provides the framework for a reconstituted analysis of the thrust and tenor of educational policies in the period discussed in Kirp's book. It allows us to see that the most dramatic change in the way such policies have been structured is not in their move away from inexplicitness to explicitness, as Kirp's account would have us believe, but in what they have been explicit about. 'Culture' and 'language' were two of the categories which dominated educational discourse and policy; let us now turn to the way these and associated themes resonated with the prevailing political and educational ideologies during this period.

DISCRIMINATION BY PROXY:

It was during the early 1960s that black students began to make some impression on the schools and classrooms in the UK's major industrial centres. These were the children of black migrants who as a reserve army of labour to the UK economy had been encouraged to leave the Caribbean and South Asia to fill the low status jobs made available in a period of economic growth and acute labour shortages. Conventional interpretations of educational policies for this period specify two main trends; first, that the goals of policy were primarily assimilationist: second, as we have seen, that in rhetoric and ideological terms these policies were racially inexplicit. Now, it may be correct to say that this is how educationists and politicians described their goals and policies; it is also true that the rhetoric of assimilation reverberated around local and national debating chambers at the time. What is most striking about the 1960s, however, and what compels our attention is the divorce of this educational rhetoric from policies and provisions in almost every other arena of social life. After all, as a number of writers have illustrated this was an era when other state policies were becoming increasingly 'race specific' (see, Carby 1982: Gilroy, 1982; Sivanandan, 1981/2). A brief summary of contemporary events and developments should be sufficient to demonstrate this point here.

The 1962 Commonwealth Immigrants Act began the process of limiting the inflow specifically of black labour. Politicians and academics may have talked about New Commonwealth migrants (or just plain 'immigrants') but this did not disguise the focus of their concern: black migrants. The key political issues at national and local level throughout the '60s crystallized around 'race' and the imposition of a colour bar, in particular, was a salient concern in areas up and down the country. For instance, studies in different parts of the country showed the extent of local political concern about colour bars in housing, in clubs and in dance halls. More generally, the extent of racial discrimination in housing and labour markets was detailed in the empirical studies summarized by William Daniel (1968) and E.J.B. Rose and his colleagues (1969). The important point here is that as citizens, as workers and as consumers of housing and leisure facilities skin colour was a defining factor for Blacks and one which emerged as a central political issue for both Blacks and Whites. The political focus upon numbers in this period made even more explicit the relationship between the migration of Blacks and the resources available to Whites.

This contrast between racially explicit policies, everyday practices and ideological assumptions, on the one hand, and the supposed inexplicitness of 'race' in educational orientations, on the other, therefore requires more careful consideration than it has usually been accorded. What might assimilation entail in this context? At a commonsense level (and often in academic treatments of the notion) assimilation is taken to mean the total absorption of one population by another, physically and/or culturally. In the 1950s and '60s it clearly did not mean physical absorption, however, as the 1949 Royal Commission on Population and various contemporary opinion polls (cited in Rose, et al 1969) testify. Intermarriage, for example, was largely discouraged by and seen as unacceptable to the white indigenous population. Similarly, there was little attempt to disrupt the residential and occupational segregation of groups designated racially different. Even in the education sphere, the growth of black school student populations and the allegedly extra pressures this placed on teachers and LEAs highlighted the 'racially-explicit' dimensions of the debate.

In this context then, several different and complex matters, generally overlooked in the extant literature, must be addressed. Was it simply the rhetorical justifications for education policies which merited the label, assimilationist, rather than the policies, per se? In the education sphere, what did assimilation denote and connote? Why did rhetorical, ideological and policy emphases in education contrast so sharply with other aspects of state policies and political emphases? And, what were the contradictions between education and other state policies? These questions, and their resolution, are of central concern in this book. Let us begin, however, with a clarification of the term, assimilation.

One of the more common ideological interpretations of this concept stresses cultural rather than physical assimilation. From this perspective, Blacks would not be seen by others or perceive themselves as a discrete group, except in terms of skin colour. This interpretation has rested on the belief that the society should be politically and culturally indivisible and that black migrants and their children should be compelled to accept established values, norms and mores. In this scenario, the educational system was necessarily ascribed a principal role in ensuring that the potentially disruptive influence of the settlement of culturally and linguistically different groups on British institutions and ways of life was minimalised swiftly. The message conveyed by governmental and advisory group documents in these years was clear: there is no place in the formal educational system for such differences and as they are dysfunctional to the smooth operation of the system they must be eradicated. Nowhere was this message stated more bluntly than in the second part of the Commonwealth Immigrants Advisory Council report:

> ... a national system of education must aim at producing citizens who can take their place in a society properly equipped to exercise rights and perform duties which are the same as other citizens. If their parents were brought up in another culture or another tradition, children should be encouraged to respect it, but a national system cannot be expected to perpetuate the different values of immigrant groups (1964, p.7).

In the words of Gordon Bowker the school had a dual function, 'that of transmitting the culture to and resocialising the immigrant child' (1968, p.82). Although the prevailing political dogma of assimilation as cultural resocialisation played a major part in defining the relationship between the educational system and black students it is important to recognise the confluence of this ideology with extant educational theories and ideologies. It was these latter theories which allowed policy-makers and practitioners to legitimate their approaches in educational terms. Of course, educational theories and ideologies are closely linked to the broader political contexts in which they are generated (Halsey, 1974), and it is important that we do not lose sight of them entirely for they provide an interpretive and legitimating framework for the translation and integration of political ideologies into educational settings.

On the face of it, cultural resocialisation is problematic in educational terms. This is partly because of the contradictions between political and educational rhetoric and the concerns we have already outlined; but also because cultural differences need to be interpreted in a way which justifies educational intervention and presents this intervention within a consensus framework of educational activity and teacher competence. An ideal way of achieving both aims is to predicate the need for assimilation on an interpretation of differences as deficits. From this stance, the processes of resocialisation, language tuition and correction, and dispersal could be argued for on the seemingly 'good' educational grounds that the culture, language and spatial concentration of black students not only impeded their educational advancement but also had the potential to affect negatively the educational progress of their white classmates.

Of course, this kind of reasoning was not new. To a greater or lesser extent it had been used to account for the relatively poorer academic performance and commitment to schooling shown by working class students in comparison with their middle class counterparts (see Baron, et al 1981). As Flude indicates, this ideologically inspired interpretation of differences allowed policy-makers to avoid questions about the legitimacy of the educational enterprise or about the structural inequalities which lead to the development of distinctive socio-cultural environments. Instead, it advances a normative conception of culture - which is White and middle class - and all other cultures are valued according to the extent to which they approximate to this social ideal. Any deviation from this norm is then designated inferior, a barrier to educability and put down to inadequate socialization. Flude goes on to say:

> The assumption is made that what goes on in school, particularly the knowledge, skills and attitudes that schools transmit, has some intrinsic value and those social class or ethnic cultures which are characterised as "deprived" do not have what it takes to adapt to the school's academic culture and values (1974, p.23).

The means by which the cultural practices and traits which deviated from this social ideal were designated deficient and inferior is clearly illustrated in the contemporary UK and USA literature of the 1960s. Here it was the family rather than the structure of opportunities available to working class Blacks and Whites which was seen as the site of oppression and the cause of educational problems. As a result, there developed a number of interventionist policies which were oriented toward alleviating the alleged cultural/linguistic deficiencies in the (black) working class and their families. Benjamin Bloom and his colleagues, amongst others, provided the intellectual lead for such interventionist policies, of which Operation Headstart in the USA was probably the most infamous. The following passage taken from their book, <u>Compensatory Education for Cultural Deprivation</u> gives a clue to the type of pathological approach which they, along with Moynihan, Coleman and Passow, provided in this period:

> In the present educational system in the United States (and elsewhere) we find a substantial group of students who do not make normal progress in their school learning. Predominantly, these are the students whose early experiences in the home, whose motivation for school learning and whose goals for the future are such as to handicap them in their schoolwork (1965, p.4).

Prescriptive analyses such as these avoided as a matter of routine the problematical and ideological nature of concepts such as 'normality' and laid the blame for any deviation from the (middle class) ideal fairly and squarely in the Black and/or working class home. This pathological interpretation was, moreover, adopted almost uncritically by urban educationists in the UK and provided the backcloth to the interventionist programmes advocated by Newsom, Plowden and others. But as critics of compensatory education pointed out, the cultural deprivation theorists succeeded in performing a significant ideological manoeuvre. By stressing the role of the family in the educative process they preserved as unproblematic the educational system and the economic, political and social context to which it both served and contributed. The name of the game in enhancing educability was attitude change either in the children (as the Newsom report suggested in 1963) or the parents (which the 1967 Plowden report emphasized).

Black students and their families in the UK were, of course, key targets for change in this ideological scenario. The pedagogic, curricular and organisational practices and orientation of the educational system were not open to debate. Instead, as the DES informed schools in 1965, the educational success of black migrant students was entirely dependent on the 'realistic understanding of the adjustments they (i.e. the students) have to make' (DES, 1965). Coming at a time when the cultural deprivation thesis was the fashion in the framing of UK social policy the DES advice to schools appeared to make 'sound educational sense' and as Jenny Williams found, schools adhered closely to the advice conveyed by central government. Teachers conceived the role of the school as a facilitating mechanism for the assimilation of black students, 'putting over a certain set of values (Christian), a code of behaviour (middle class) and a set of academic and job aspirations in which white collar jobs have higher prestige than manual, clean jobs than dirty...' (1967, p.237).

The point we want to stress here is that the translation of assimilationist imperatives into educational prescriptions and practices did not require the explicit use of 'racial', or more accurately, racist categorizations or concepts. Rather, non-racist (or deracialised) criteria were invoked as the legitimating grounds for action. Covertly, however, derogatory evaluations and classifications of groups ascribed in racial terms were made, as indeed they needed to be if assimilationist ideas were to be seen to 'work'. And these allowed for the differential and discriminatory treatment of black students.

The key to this version of assimilationist ideology and an integral constituent of the nascent resocialisation programme was language tuition. As Bowker wrote in 1968: '"Linguistic integration", it is accepted, is a necessary precondition of social integration. Certainly a child's inability to speak English presents any school with a major obstacle, not only to the transmission of culture but to resocialisation as well' (1969, p.75). His comments certainly reflected the propositions advanced regularly by Schools Council and DES documents and research reports of the period. In 1967, for instance, the Schools Council maintained that the teaching of English was important not only to enable the student 'to communicate satisfactorily and adequately in an English-speaking community' but also and 'equally important ... to provide through language the means whereby the child becomes part of his (sic) community - to provide the key to cultural and social assimilation' (1967, pp.3-4). Nor did the DES dissent from this position. Reporting in 1971 it suggested that black students were at a continual disadvantage because their homes did little to 'reduce the adverse effects of inadequacies of language. Many children go home to hear either their native tongue spoken or a form of pidgin English. Against a background of this kind the best intentions of the schools can easily be almost nullified' (1971, p.65). Unless, of course, the intentions of the school had been geared toward bi-lingualism. Faced with a growing number of students who spoke either no English or a variant of Standard English distinguished by its own distinctive grammar and phonetics, the establishment of bi-lingual or multi-lingual programmes was, in principle at least, a plausible alternative. Why the different languages of black students were not accepted positively as a basis for the implementation of bi-lingual programmes in the school can be accounted for easily. First, because it contradicted this educationally focussed interpretation of assimilation. Assimilation was not negotiable, neither was it a two-way process; after all, if black parents and students were allowed to retain any identifiable affiliation with their country of origin then 'certain parts of the curriculum, especially the learning of English, may be thought of as irrelevant' (Bowker, 1968, p.47). As we said earlier, assimilation demanded a denial of affiliations to any other cultural, linguistic or national identities: a point made brutally, but succinctly, in 1964 by the former Conservative MP for Southall:

> I feel that Sikh parents should encourage their children to give up their turbans, their religion and their dietary laws. If they refuse to integrate then we must be tough. They must be told they would be the first to go if there was unemployment and it should be a condition of being given National Assistance that the immigrants go to English classes (quoted in Bagley, 1973, p.304).

Second, bi-lingualism was not considered seriously as a policy goal because there were educational theories which, on the face of it, rejected the view that bi-lingualism was an asset. Thus drawing selectively on Basil Bernstein's theories of socio-lingusitics, the DES asserted:

> If there is any validity in Bernstein's view that the restricted code of many culturally deprived children may hinder their ability to develop certain kinds of thinking, it is certainly applicable to non-English speaking immigrant children who may be suffering, not only from a limitation of a restricted code in their own language, but from the complication of trying to learn a second language. Experiencing language difficulties, they may be suffering handicaps which are not conspicuous because they concern the very structure of thought... The bilingual situation can be a very bewildering one for immigrant children and can produce within them a sense of psychological and emotional insecurity (DES, 1971, p.9).

A favourable interpretation of this pasage would claim that it was based on diagnostic accounts of students' competence in their first language; at worst, and more likely, it was simply wild speculation. It had no empirical backing but stemmed from a racist assessment of these languages. To this extent, the DES merely seconded what the Schools Council had asserted in 1967; namely, that it did not encourage schools to pursue a policy of bi-lingualism except 'where it is a case of language generally accepted as a foreign language for school purposes in England, such as Italian...' (1967, p.6). Put bluntly, modern and classical European languages were legitimate elements of the formal curriculum; the languages spoken in black countries were not. This undeniably racist proposition had another, equally insidious dimension, however. That is, the languages spoken by black students were seen to denote, per se, their linguistic and verbal deprivation. Educationally, therefore, students should be discouraged from using them because they impeded their intellectual and social development! Once again we see how deracialised concepts and themes (in this case language deprivation) were used to describe and rationalise a racist posture.

It was also possible to discern a racist impulse in the allocation of resources for English as a Second Language (ESL) tuition. Without doubt, ESL provision was the most obvious policy response to the presence of black students in UK schools in the 1960s, in terms of the deployment of human and financial resources. But these resources were allocated in a highly selective manner. Whilst it was impossible to deny that students of South Asian origin needed ESL tuition, those of Afro-Caribbean origin apparently presented a more dubious case. It was 'authoritatively' argued that Afro-Caribbean students spoke a sloppy, broken English variously called 'patois', 'creole' or 'dialect'. As a result, few LEAs, or for that matter the DES, considered Afro-Caribbean students in need of English language provision; the authenticity and legitimacy of the language was summarily dismissed. What these students needed, it was asserted, was language correction. In his survey of how LEAs up and down the country had responded to the inflow of black students into local schools H.E.R. Townsend found that within a generally variegated picture of provision, 'One of the points of similarity of the arrangements for the teaching of English... has been the fact that few West Indian pupils were found to be in full- or part-time language centres or classes' (1971, p.49). Creole was seen as akin to Bernstein's notion of a restricted code, a designation which not only ignored the language's inherent logical structure and coherence but which also led to the stigmatization in education settings both of the language itself and its users (Edwards, 1979). In the words of Arthur Brittan and Mary Maynard: 'To remove patois from its cultural milieu and treat it as bad English is racist. Failure to take account of patois within the educational process is to make that process itself biased' (1984, p.163).

This discussion of the importance which the DES and LEAs ascribed to language provision (and correction) exemplifies both the interpretation of assimilation which we have outlined and the way this interpretation was presented within a deracialised framework. The use of class based rather than specifically racial theories to support the claim that cultural resocialisation was necessary for the realisation of equality of opportunity not only attracted the support of educationists but also served as a bulwark to alternative interpretations and approaches. But what was hidden behind this approach was the important point that differentiation and discrimination operated on the assumption that the cultures and languages of black migrants and their children were inferior. According to this reasoning then they had the potential to block the assimilationist process and the educational advancement of the students. In fact we would argue that the denigration of black cultures and languages was allowed to proceed unchallenged and become part of the conventional wisdom in the debate about 'the education of coloured immigrants' precisely because it deployed non-racial criteria. The substitution of fashionable and apparently legitimate educational concepts and categories allowed these discriminatory processes to operate almost with impunity. A clear case of discrimination by proxy.

DISPERSAL: 'A SYSTEM OF SOCIAL ENGINEERING'?

The spatial concentration of black migrants and their children in the inner areas of the UK's major industrial cities provides another example of the contradictions between state policies in education and other aspects of social policy, in this case housing. With one or two notable exceptions, such as Birmingham (Flett, 1981), local authorities did at best nothing to disrupt these residential patterns and, at worst, actually encouraged and exacerbated them. The response from educational policy-makers was of an entirely different nature, however. They saw spatial concentration as a barrier to the realisation of their assimilationist goals. At the same time, white parents complained vociferously to local and central government representatives about the emergence of 'black-majority' schools. The confluence of these pressures resulted ultimately in DES support for dispersal, of which bussing constituted an important element. In its circular of June 1965, the DES sanctioned the forced removal of black students qua black students from their local schools into schools in other parts of the LEA where, it was argued, their contact with white students and the 'majority culture' would be enhanced. On the face of it, DES endorsement of bussing marked a departure from its general policy. At the same time it is important to acknowledge the similarities. First, and in contrast to Kirp's facile claim that bussing had 'no deep ideological roots' (1979, p.73) the policy was firmly embedded in the assimilationist mould. Second, it retained a commitment to deracialisation by deploying proxy explanatory concepts in support of its action. As the Department emphasised defiantly in 1971: 'The only ground for dispersal suggested by Circular 7/65 was educational need. To approach this matter on racial grounds would...be contrary to educational tradition...' (1971, p.20). So what were these perceived educational needs? In its passage on 'Spreading the Children' in its 7/65 circular to LEAs, the DES put it in the following terms. First, '...as the proportion of immigrant children in a school or class increases, the problems will become more difficult to solve and the chances of assimilation more remote' (1965, p.4). Hardly, then, a response to perceived educational needs; more an elucidation and implementation of a political ideology. Nor did many people believe seriously that increased contact between black and white students would facilitate the development of 'harmonious race relations'. On the contrary, as one M.P. admitted to the 1973 Select Committee on Race Relations and Immigration: '... I should be very surprised if we ever thought it (i.e. bussing) was ever worth doing in order to produce a "mix" of children which might perhaps inculcate a greater understanding of inter-racial problems'. Against this admission, the claim of one Bradford LEA administrator that: 'Dispersal is...quite simply a system of social engineering' which would help white students accept their black counterparts 'into their school society as equals' had rather a hollow ring to it (quoted in Rex, Troyna and Naguib, 1983, p.95). Indeed, if there was a grain of truth in this philosophy then, at the very least, black and white students would have been equal candidates for removal - and they were not.

Later in circular 7/65 the DES offered other 'educational' rationales for the policy:

> Experience suggests however that apart from unusual difficulties (such as a high proprotion of non-English speakers), up to a fifth of immigrant children in any group fit in with reasonable ease, but that, if the proportion goes over about one-third either in the school as a whole or in any one class, serious strains arise (1965, p.8).

Put another way, the DES was ostensibly concerned with, first, the language needs of 'ncn-English speakers'; second, the potentially deleterious impact of a relatively large proportion of black students on the educational progress of white students; and third, the pressure exerted by teacher unions and LEAs who complained about the professional and financial stresses they experienced in coping with the new (black) immigrants. The first two concerns were predicated on spurious grounds and their relationship with bussing policies, illogical. To begin with, if the language needs of students were a legitimate cause for concern then language not skin colour would have been used to decide which students were eligible for bussing. But they were not. Instead as David Milner observes: '"Immigrant" children were dispersed, irrespective of whether they were recently immigrant or not, irrespective of whether they had language difficulties or not, and this included some West Indian children (who, in contrast to what we now know, were then thought not to have language difficulties)' (1983, p.199). Secondly, to propose that the presence of black students, regardless of their proportionate number, would affect detrimentally the educational performance of white students was unashamedly racist. And, as later research carried out both in the UK (Little, 1975) and the USA (St. John, 1975) was to demonstrate, it was empirically incorrect. There were never any tenable educational grounds for dispersal; there were, however, numerous educational arguments against this policy. It contravened, for example, one of the general principles enshrined in the 1944 Education Act; namely, that as far as possible 'pupils are to be educated in accordance with the wishes of their parents' (section 76, p.56). The wishes of black parents in LEAs such as Ealing, Bradford, West Bromwich and Wolverhampton were never consulted however (see Killian, 1979 and Weintraub, 1972 for specific details on local dispersal arrangements). In fact, even when the Race Relations Board intervened in the debate surrounding bussing in Ealing the views of black parents and their children were not sought. As the Board's assessor, Maurice Kogan, put it in his report:

> It was not possible within my schedule of visits, nor was it implicit in the terms of reference given to me informally by the Board's officers, that I should meet the parents of children subject to the dispersal arrangements in order to ascertain their

feelings about the arrangements.... I saw a few Asian parents at the Reception Centre in Southall Town Hall but did not speak with them (Kogan, 1975, p.3).

The LEAs and DES also overlooked the substantial research (some of which the DES had commissioned) which pointed to the educational benefits associated with neighbourhood and community schooling. By forcibily removing black students from their local schools, LEAs, with the duplicity of the DES, effectively prevented anything beyond minimal contact between black parents and their children's schools.

To contend that the dispersal of black students was premised on 'the grounds of educational need' was both cynical and deceitful. The reality shows that it was based purely and simply on the grounds of political expediency: to assuage the anxieties of white parents that central and local government was doing all it could to assimilate black students without disrupting the education of white students. It was no coincidence that the following was the only italicized passage in DES circular 7/65:

It will be helpful if the parents of non-immigrant children see that practical measures have been taken to deal with the problems in the schools, and that the progress of their own children is not being restricted by the undue preoccupation of the teaching staff with the linguistic and other difficulties of immigrant children (1965, p.9).

EQUAL RIGHTS?

Dispersal exemplified in the crudest possible way DES commitment to its 1965 stance: that assimilation would be achieved once the black communities apprehended a 'realistic understanding of the adjustments they have to make'. The deracialisation of dispersal policies and the attending debate clearly facilitated this process by providing alternative concepts and premises for the justification and implementation of racist-inspired proposals. But we have shown that dispersal was neither a legitimate nor logical response to perceived educational needs. It was a policy of surrender to racism. Something which showed such contemptuous disregard for black parents and their children could not be described in any other terms. This denial of the equal rights of black citizens was commented on by a spokesperson for Ealing Community Relations Council who insisted that whilst bussing might serve the assimilationist impulse it ruled out of court the views and demands of black citizens. What right, he asked, did white politicians and policy-makers have to 'over-ride the identity and culture of a minority within a multicultural society'? (quoted in Killian, 1979, p.203). Such a question threw into sharp relief not only the enforced political subordination of black citizens in Britain but also the clear failure of politicians and policy-makers to adhere to Roy Jenkins oft-quoted remark of 1966 that the national aim was 'not a flattening process of assimilation but an equal opportunity accompanied by cultural diversity, in an atmosphere of mutual tolerance' (quoted in Patterson, 1969, p.113). Although this vague prescription presaged changes more in political rhetoric than practice, nevertheless it has been seen by some analysts, rightly or wrongly, as a symbolic marker: a time when assimilationist zeal receded and integrationist ideals gained prominence. What is perhaps most significant regarding this advice was that a prominent government spokesperson (Jenkins was then Home Secretary), for the first time, had acknowledged publicly that black citizens did not enjoy equal rights in the U.K. In the next few years a plethora of research data was to bear incontrovertible witness to this fact. In 1967, for instance, the PEP survey into racial discrimination in England highlighted just how far racialism defined the quality of life experienced by the black communities, despite the Labour government's 1965 anti-discrimination law. 'In employment, housing and the provision of services', wrote William Daniel in his summary of the survey findings, 'there is racial discrimination varying in extent from the massive to the substantial' (1968, p.209). We have already seen how racialism also operated in the educational system, covertly and overtly. On top of this was evidence that black students were more likely than their white colleagues to be consigned to the lower academic streams of the secondary school and to schools for the Educationally Sub-Normal (ESN). In the light of this evidence, Jenkins' demand for equal opportunities seemed to have fallen on deaf ears.

By the end of the 1960s, beginning of the 1970s, there were signs that there was no longer a general acceptance of assimilation as cultural resocialisation. The new rhetoric of integration espoused by Jenkins was competing for recognition and space on the educational policy agenda. But certain aspects of the earlier versions of assimilation remained non-negotiable and impervious to change, especially the process and direction of adaptation, as the following assertion from the 1973 Select Committee on Race Relations and Immigration report testifies: 'Those who come to settle must, to some extent, accept the ways of the country in which they are going to live and of whose society they form a part' (1973, p.23). The 'extent' was, of course, not a matter for negotiation but one for white policy-makers and politicians to determine. What had changed, however, was a perception and understanding of how assimilation could best be realised. In short, what occurred was a re-appraisal of strategy. So how do we account for the demise of 'unity through (culutral) genocide' and the ascendancy of 'unity through (cultural) diversity' as the organising principle of race-related educational initiatives?

During the 1970s, researchers concerned with the educational experiences of black students began to question the primacy of cultural deprivation theories. Analyses which highlighted, amongst other things, the differential allocation and treatment of black students in the educational system, the racist imagery conveyed through teaching aids and materials and Anglocentric assumptions of the formal and hidden curriculum, suggested major faults in the school as a socialising institution. This new genre of studies blended a concern with the supposed cultural deficiencies of Blacks (and, by implication, their culpability in the problems they experienced in school) with a consideration of the alienating and dysfunctional features of school life. This helped to spark off a new trend toward curriculum reform and new models of educational experience. But it was given greater urgency by critical political events and considerations. With one eye on the recent 'race riots' in the USA, educational policy-makers, amongst others, recognised the need for strategic changes in their race-related approaches if they were to avert similar disturbances in the U.K. The 1969 Select Committee on Race Relations and Immigration provided a stimulus for change in its report, The Problems of Coloured School Leavers. Here, black youths - and especially those of Afro-Caribbean origin - were typified as a 'social time bomb' which was likely to be detonated in the continuing absence of 'equal treatment with their white contemporaries'. It went on to warn that: 'Unless they get this treatment the seeds of racial discord may be sewn' (1969, p.7). The priority, then, was to convince black students of the 'pay-off' which derived from an involvement in the school and the credentials it had to offer. The means by which this would be achieved would be through the provision of,

> ...teaching about the countries from which the immigrants in any particular town came. Here material direct from those countries can be displayed in the classroom by immigrant children. Children in primary schools in Hackney or Brixton, for example, could be taught West Indian songs, or children in Wolverhampton be shown Indian art, jewellery and costumes. This would help bring immigrant children into the life of the school (1969, pp.41-42).

At the same time,

> Deliberate efforts should also be made to teach newly arrived immigrants about life in this country - our customs, social conventions and industrial activities as well as our language (1969, p.42).

Let us look closely at both the assumptions and programmatic features of this integrationist perspective. To begin with, the Select Committee's proposals bear testimony to our earlier claim that the shift to integrationist ideals did not entail an ideological break with the past. Assimilation remained the goal; what differed in this scenario was a recognition that assimilation could only be acheived successfully with the compliance of black students; thus the need to 'bring immigrant children into the life of the school'. The concession to a minimal and conditional cultural diversity in schools can only be seen as a pre-emptive strike; to counteract black resistance and ensure that disquiet about the educational experiences of black students did not boil over either into a full-scale secession from the mainstream education services (something which was feared in the

ILEA as we shall see in the following chapter) or into serious disorders on the streets, as had happened in the USA. The political slogan was alienation; once again, a concept used differentially in selected contexts but one which had an educational resonance linking it to reformist notions of child-centredness and culturally relevant curricula. It also acted as a twin concept to 'underachievement'. In political terms, then, the consequences of alienation could be seen as militancy and rebellion. In educational terms they connoted underachievement and allowed for the amelioration of the latter (underachievement) as a way of forestalling the former (rebellion). As with cultural resocialisation, underachievement provided a professional task for teachers. But, at the same time it failed to make explicit the class bases of the phenomenon. It also circumvented the volitional and rational responses of black students to the deficit effects of racism. From this vantage point, Robert Jeffcoate's claim that multiculturalism (as the later variant of integrationist ideals and practices) evolved in response to the educational needs of black students is simply fatuous (1984a, p.180). Justice had to be seen to be done and as policies such as bussing had been initiatied simply to appease the racist sentiments of certain white communities so 'complementary' policies to assuage the anxieties of black parents also had to be introduced. The formation of the Black Students' Action Collective (Black Sac) in a South London school in 1974 and the growth of black supplementary schools in London and elsewhere around this time exemplified Blacks' discontent with schooling and their reluctance to engage, more than in a perfunctory manner, with its routines and disciplines. Such opposition needed to be nipped in the bud.

It is also clear that the Select Committee did not see its package of prescribed reforms either as relevant to all schools or as appropriate in all levels of the formal curriculum. On the first point, the Select Committee regarded schools in ethnically mixed areas, such as Brixton, Haringey and Wolverhampton, as the site for changes; a conception of reform, therefore, that not only confined and defined the parameters of change but which also reaffirmed the need for such schools to play a prominent assimilationist and anglicising role with regard to their black students. The recent research of Little and Willey (1981) and Troyna and Ball (1983) has shown that teachers in ethnically homogeneous schools rarely depart from this advice and continue to regard multicultural and antiracist education as irrelevant to their particular context and student population (see chapter 6). On the second point, the Select Committee clearly did not see its proposals as a basis for change in all areas of the formal curriculum. In fact, its comments were directed only at primary schools; it seems reasonable to infer that in the secondary school any comparable changes would take place in the low-status, non-credentialling parts of the curriculum.

It seems to us that the Select Committee report, along with other contemporary documents and reports on this theme, did not promote integration/multiculturalist perspectives as a legitimate educational orthodoxy which had implications for all LEAs and schools. Rather, the report's recommendations constituted a 'knee-jerk' reflex to actual and anticipated disquiet about the education and life chances of black students. In fact such crude attempts at crisis-management were to figure prominently in offical reports throughout the 1970s, an observation also made by Andy Green: 'The potential danger of resistance and dissent amongst black youth is the recurrent leitmotif running through all DES, select committee and schools council documents on multicultural education and black children at school' (1982, p.23). After 1981 such apprehensions gained an extra veracity and urgency.

SARIS, SAMOSAS AND STEEL BANDS:

Perhaps most significantly in the context of our general argument is that the integrationist, then multiculturalist/cultural pluralist models of educational change retained the deracialised form of discourse and reflected, at the same time, the educational system's unswerving commitment to forms of assimilation. The official agenda was framed so that 'the problem' of black students and not the problems confronted by black students became the rationale for policy intervention. The package of reforms introduced in the 1970s under the generic label, multicultural education, was construed first and foremost as a series of palliatives. The aim: to make the educational experience of black students more palatable. Racism, in other words, as a structural feature of the UK educational system was not challenged; neither was its profound and fundamental effect on the life chances of black students brought into the official debate. Instead, culture retained its status as the key explanatory concept. Life-styles and not life chances was the fulcrum around which the multicultural education initiatives of the 1970s operated. Throughout these years the official state agenda promoted and endorsed what Kogila Moodley (in the context of Canada's multicultural ideology) has termed 'a festive aura of imaginary consensus' (1983 p.320). The 3 Ss (saris, samosas and steel bands) interpretation of cultural pluralism was advanced as the operational mode through which the 3 Rs (resistance, rejection and rebellion) would be contained and defused. Such a formulation could only be explicable in terms of assimilationist imperatives. So according to Eric Bolton in his discussion of the factors which supposedly contributed to the rise of cultural pluralist objectives in education:

> The most powerful drive has come from the growing belief that an individual needs to be secure in his (sic) own culture, and to see that culture respected by others if he is to be confident and competent in a new society and if he is to move out of the ghetto and into the mainstream of ordinary life (1979, p.6 Emphasis added).

This emphasis on the suppression of cultural differences as contrary to the ultimate goal of assimilation was also commented on in a Home Office report:

For the curriculum to have meaning and relevance for all pupils now in our schools, its content, emphasis and the values and assumptions contained must reflect the wide range of cultures, histories and life styles in our multi-racial society (1978, p.6).

In order for the state's definition of 'the problem' to retain credibility and support dissenting voices had to be kept off the official agenda, especially if they called into question the way schools legitimate routinely inequalities between groups designated racially different. In this context it is not surprising that the Secretary of State for Education (then Mark Carlisle) made it clear when setting up the Rampton (now Swann) Commttee that he would not consider any recommendations which challenged existing educational structures. The fate of two, fairly recent reports commissioned by the Schools Council also demonstrates our point. The first of these, Education for a Multiracial Society, should have been published in 1978 but only appeared in censored form in 1981 - censored because its authors attempted to widen their original terms of reference and incorporate material which showed 'how prevalent racist attitudes are in schools and in the rest of society' (Hodges, 1978, p.10). Dawn Gill's report Assessment in a Multicultural Society: Geography met with similar resistance from the Schools Council and was rejected for publication. Once again this was because of the author's attempt to widen the original brief outlined in her contract. This had said:

The purposes of the commissioned studies is to investigate how syllabuses and examinations at 16+ can meet the needs of all pupils in a multicultural society. The steering group recognizes that the broad notion of multiculture includes cultural groups arising from sex, class, regional and other differences; however, this activity (i.e. the project) is confining itself only to those aspects of diversity which have a religious, linguistic or ethnic base.

In the event, Dawn Gill eschewed this defining and confining perspective in her report and centralised the debilitating impact of racism on black students' life chances - a phenomenon which would not be overcome simply through the recognition and celebration of cultural diversity and life styles in the examination syllabus. As Gill insisted in the first few pages of her report:

Examination courses which ensure better grades for non whites will not necessarily have any effect on discrimination in employment. Unless there is an attempt in schools to educate against racism the result of ensuring that examinations better serve the needs of ethnic minority candidates could be an increased percentage of overqualified, unemployed or poorly paid non white people (1982, p.5).

Put another way, racism and not formal educational qualifications is the main determinant of life chances for black students in the UK, a fact heavily stressed in research reports (Troyna and Smith, 1983 for example) but which continues to be ignored in the formulation of educational policies. The claim in the 1981 report, Racial Disadvantage, that: 'It has long been evident that we have not got ethnic minority education right' exemplifies the misconceived and ideologically slanted basis of educational policy intervention. What Gill and others are saying is that the state's avowed commitment to equality of opportunity in school and post-school life will remain a sham until the structure of opportunities available to black students are challenged and dismantled. The aims and objectives of multicultural education programmes are premised along precisely the same lines as their ideological forerunners. They are geared to a perspective which sees education as the main distributor of life chances; they are also committed to the belief that black students must be persuaded to accept the meritocratic function and credibility of schooling. The typification of national policies and debates as exemplars of a deracialisation process, rather than as racially inexplicit, allows us to conclude that the ideological apparatus on which such interventions have been based constitutes a diversion of genuine egalitarian policy. By obfuscating the realities of racism as a genuinely divisive fact of life in the UK the deracialisation process helps to sustain an ideological facade of equality of opportunity.

Chapter Two

MULTICULTURAL EDUCATION IN ACTION: THE
DERACIALISATION OF POLICIES IN INNER LONDON AND
MANCHESTER

It is tempting to assume on a priori grounds, that the national
patterns and trends in race-related matters in education in the 1960s
and '70s were faithfully and automatically reproduced in the thinking
and practices of LEAs up and down the country. However, partly
because of the vagaries of local politics, partly also because of the
structural decentralisation of the UK's educational system we should
be cautious in making such an assumption. On this second point, it is
important to note that even in the face of the current trend towards
centralisation, LEAs still retain some scope in determining what goes
on in their schools. In the sphere of race relations it could be
contended that they enjoy greater discretionary powers than in most
other curricular and pedagogic matters. As we have seen, for
instance, the DES has been at best permissive, at worst ambivalent in
the advice it has prescribed and circulated on this theme. The local
response to DES support for bussing is a good example of how LEAs
may or may not follow centrally-produced advice. As the department
noted in 1971, the impact of its circular on bussing was patchy, to say
the least: 'Some have adopted a policy of dispersing immigrant
children, but the majority have not, either because it was
impracticable or because they did not agree with it' (1971, p.18).
Interestingly, central government has often referred to its own lack
of authority in this decentralised system as the main reason for the
absence of a national educational policy on race-related matters. For
example, replying to the Select Committee's recommendation that a
central fund be established to which LEAs could apply for 'resources
to meet the special needs of black pupils', the Home Office had this
to say:

> The public provision of education is, for the most part, the
> responsibility of the local education authorities. It is financed
> like any other local authority service largely through the rates
> and the Rate Support Grant. It is the job of the local authority
> to decide how best to use its resources of staff and money to
> meet the needs of its area. If specific grants for particular
> aspects of education in which local authorities have previously

enjoyed discretion were to be introduced, the effect might be to reduce the scope of local responsibility (Home Office, 1974, pp.13-14).

We have profound reservations about the general legitimacy of this argument and elsewhere Troyna has shown how central government's claims about institutional powerlessness are invoked and utilised only when it is politically expedient for it to do so (Troyna, 1982; Dorn and Troyna, 1982). Nevertheless such claims are not entirely untenable and notwithstanding current moves toward an emphasis on the national rather than local character of the education service, LEAs (and their schools) continue to command some say over the thrust and nature of their provisions.

Against this background, it is important to scrutinise empirically how far central government's determination to deracialise educational debates and policy in the 1960s and 1970s also characterised LEA approaches in this period. Naturally in a decentralised system, variations in approach and provision are to be expected. We are concerned here, however, with the conceptual frameworks within which LEAs situated their provision. In this context we shall confine our analysis to two LEAs: Inner London (ILEA) and Manchester.(1) We have chosen these Authorities partly for pragmatic reasons, partly also because they are exemplary of a development of thinking in racial matters which was to be replicated in a number of other LEAs.

To begin with the pragmatic grounds for this selection. In the late 1960s, and especially during the '70s, a number of Authorities in a variety of circumstances had drafted documents on race relations. These tended, however, to be position papers confined to specific issues such as English as a Second Language or bussing. Clearly one could infer general educational and race-related principles from these documents; even so, they were, to all intents and purposes, specific policies or advisory notes in response to immediate contingencies. The policy statements produced by the ILEA in 1977 and in Manchester in 1980, were of an entirely different nature. These were general affirmations of the notion of multicultural education which had the support of the respective Education Committees and which were (eventually) circulated to LEA employees (mainly senior teaching staff). Those who drafted these statements conceived of them as change-agents; their aim: to provide a reconstituted conceptual framework for curricular, organisational and pedagogic procedures. Whether or not they achieved these goals is a different question and not of immediate concern here (but see Troyna and Ball, 1983; 1985b). The point we want to stress is that they were of a distinctly different status from other contemporary educational documents on this theme produced either within or beyond the two Authorities.

We also see these policy documents as exemplary models for other LEAs; that is to say, neither the concerns they addressed nor the solutions they proposed were unique. Both operationalised specific interpretations of cultural pluralism in response to locally perceived and interpreted problems through which racial issues impinged on local politics and educational institutions. They may both be designated, therefore, as classic examples of deracialisation although the ways in which this process was operationalised differed. What is more, policy-makers in both LEAs accepted uncritically many of the key assumptions which over the years have become, in the words of Brian Bullivant, 'part of the rhetoric and conventional wisdom of multicultural education' (1981, p.237). It is important to make this point clear if the case studies which follow are to be seen as more than merely descriptive accounts. The conceptual tools utilised by ILEA and Manchester policy-makers, the assumptions which underpinned their policies and the reformist programmes which stemmed from them together constitute some of the ways in which multicultural education approaches have typically been developed both in the UK and elsewhere.

THE RHETORIC OF MULTICULTURAL EDUCATION:

'Very few theories can have suffered so short an optimistic phase as those concerned with multiracial education' remarked Williams in the early 1980s (1981, p.221). A number of reasons may be adduced for this, but at least part of the explanation has to do with the assumptions used routinely to underpin multicultural education initiatives and the dubious claims made about their efficacy. Bullivant's empirical study of multicultural education ideologies and programmes in six countries in the 1970s led him to specify three 'key assumptions' which demonstrate our point. These are:

(a) that by learning about his (sic) cultural and ethnic "roots" an ethnic child will improve his educational achievement;

(b) the closely related claim that learning about his culture, its traditions and so on will improve equality of opportunity;

(c) that learning about other cultures will reduce children's (and adult) prejudice and discrimination towards those from different cultural and ethnic backgrounds (1981, p.236).

These propositions constitute, more or less, the grounds on which proposals from the DES, Schools Council and various Select Committees were based in the 1960s and 1970s. They also figure prominently in the Rampton/Swann Committee's 1981 interim report. And it is not difficult to see why they are attractive to educationists and policy-makers. To begin with, all three propositions crystallize around the notion of equality of opportunity. The first two propositions also appeal to a commonsense belief in the desirability of child-centred approaches in enhancing the educability of students, and to the role of educational credentials in determining the occupational and life chances of students, irrespective of their class, gender or ethnic backgrounds. Margaret Gibson (1976) has specified these two propositions as the underlying conceptual basis for the 'Benevolent Multiculturalism' model of educational change. The conditions which give rise to this model, writes Gibson, are 'the continuing academic failure of students from a certain minority ethnic group whose school performance continues to lag behind national norms' (1976, p.7). In accounting for these differences in performance 'benevolent multiculturalists' minimise cultural and genetic deficit interpretations and promote, instead, educational programmes designed to ensure greater compatibility between the students' home and school cultures. Simply put, the aim is to improve academic performance in order to provide equality of opportunity; the target population for these reformist strategies is the discrete group of 'underachieving' students; the strategy: the provision and availability of a culturally relevant curriculum and teaching aids. Bullivant's third proposition is also attractive to educationists because it rests on the grounds that what goes on during a student's '15,000 hours' in school has the potential to counteract the divisive influences which s/he may confront outside the school gates. Put differently, it resonates with the widely-held belief that education is a main contributor to social change. Gibson characterises programmes based on this belief as the 'Cultural Understanding' approach. Unlike the particularistic concerns of 'Benevolent Multiculturalism' this model is universalistic in its thrust. It is an inclusive approach which is intended to implicate all students in the process of re-appraisal and change, regardless of their ethnic origin.

The analytical and conceptual distinctions drawn by Gibson are apposite to our discussion of policy developments in the ILEA and Manchester. We want to argue that the 'Benevolent Multiculturalism' model depicts the approach taken in London whilst the path followed by Manchester policy-makers approximates to the 'Cultural Understanding' model. But systematizing the approaches is only half the story; we also need to know why a particular model of educational change assumed pre-eminence over others. Further, why change along multicultural lines was even considered by policy-makers in these two Authorities. To answer these questions we need to reconstruct the local events and developments which impinged on the consciousness of local professional officers and elected members in the two Authorities and which persuaded them to disavow previous and alternative educational principles. Let's begin with the ILEA.

THE ILEA: A CASE OF 'BENEVOLENT MULTICULTURALISM':

London has always been one of the main settlement areas for migrants into this country, a pattern which continued with the infusion of migrants from the UK's colonies and ex-colonies in the Caribbean and South Asia after the second world war. In the early 1970s, Townsend and Brittan reported that of the 270,745 students defined as 'immigrant' by the DES in 1971, slightly over half attended schools in London (1972). But despite this long history of an ethnically mixed student population, the Authority did little until 1977 to encourage its teaching and administrative staff to take this factor into account in appraising their practices and procedures. Asked about the ILEA's stance on this issue before 1977, a local Community Relations Officer put it like this: 'Before the 1977 policy it was a case of nondiscrimination, that we treat everybody equally.

We are all God's children, that kind of approach'. Raymond Giles' interviews with the headteachers and staff in various ILEA schools in the mid-1970s reaffirms this general characterisation:

> Many heads and teachers did not favour multiracial approaches to education, nor did they feel that children should be seen or treated any differently because of race or colour. Many schools with this philosophy were in favour of cultural assimilation as an educational goal (1977, p.96).

A critical feature in this trend toward cultural assimilation was, of course, language provision for students whose mother tongue was not English. In this respect the ILEA followed assiduously national thinking and practice. Its provision was confined to first stage ESL tuition for students from South Asia; students of Afro-Caribbean origin, on the other hand, were omitted entirely from the programme. The aim then, was to provide non-English speaking students with functional competence in English, a provision which would facilitate their adaptation to the UK education service and, at the same time, help to ensure that the meritocratic credibility of that service remained intact. Put bluntly, it was incumbent on the students to adapt to the system, rather than the other way round - a mode of thinking which, as we saw in the previous chapter, characterised national policy approaches.

In the ILEA this conception received the benediction of Eric Briault, Education Officer of the Authority between 1971-1977. His influential document, <u>An Education Service for the Whole Community</u>, written in 1973, reflected a commitment to a community-oriented education service. While he recognised that 'any future provision' in the ILEA 'must be based on the existence of a multiracial society' he failed to specify either the conceptual basis of any such provision or the strategies which might be developed in line with this prescription. In fact, his concern was little more than rhetoric; only one other allusion was made to this theme in the 64 page report and, significantly, this appeared in the section, 'Special Problems'. Here he alerted his readers to the educational implications of social disadvantage and went on to say:

> Recent immigrants present difficulties of language, insufficient education before arrival, and problems of settling into a strange urban way of life. Their different outlook and background constitute a special challenge to teachers (1973, p.19).

Clearly, Briault's diagnosis rested on the assumption that any problems in ethnically-mixed schools derived either from the recent arrival of migrant students or from deeply embedded cultural differences. Either way they were explicable mainly in terms of migration: they were transient problems which, with the help of the school, would disappear with the passage of time. From this vantage point, the availability of ESL teaching, a continued commitment to conventional teaching materials, methods and curriculum and patience were all that were requested of the system.

The priority accorded to this form of assimilation within the ILEA was also reflected in the way responsibility for race-related matters was delegated within the inspectorate. Between 1966-1974 responsibility rested with one person and comprised only part of his brief as Inspector for the Socially and Culturally Deprived - a title which, in itself denoted the prevailing mode of conceptual thought within the Authority. It was not until 1974 that an Inspector for Community Relations was appointed, a move prompted as much by political as educational motives. The holder of the post previously had been head of English at a school in Brixton where, in direct response to growing unrest amongst black students, he had helped to initiate a Black Studies course. He recalled that his initial brief as an inspector had been broadly defined but that, essentially, he was expected 'to look at issues related to black kids at school and to work on the question of liaison consultation with communities'. He also recognised the political imperatives associated with his appointment: 'being crude, I suspect (my appointment) can also be seen as a concern over lack of achievement and the problems of behaviour'. These were indeed issues which were attracting increasing attention in the Authority during the 1970s and which, more or less, precipitated the publication of the ILEA's policy statement on multiethnic education in 1977.

During the late 1960s the Authority's Research and Statistics (R and S) group initiated a longitudinal study of a cohort of students born in London between 1959-60. The students were tested on their reading attainment on four occasions in their school career, the first in 1968 when they were 8+ years old. In 1975, Alan Little (formerly Director of the R and S group) reported on the combined results of the 1968 literacy survey and a related project also carried out in ILEA schools which had looked at a range of other abilities. One of his four main conclusions was that:

> The relatively poor performance of minority pupils is across the curriculum (passive and active vocabulary, verbal reasoning, reading, Englsh, mathematics, and study skills) although some differences can be found in certain parts of the curriculum. Finally, under-privileged white children perform at a higher level than West Indian settlers and this appears to be true of pupils before and in the early years of their primary education (1975, p.68).

This apparent trend towards the 'educational underachievement' of Black, especially Afro-Caribbean students had another dimension which had first been brought to light in an internal Authority report in 1966. This showed that while 'immigrant' students constituted only 13.2 per cent of the ILEA's primary and secondary school populations, 23.3 per cent of students in the Authority's ESN schools were of 'immigrant', largely Afro-Caribbean, origin. These data assumed an even more insidious meaning when in 1967 an ILEA survey reported that teachers in ESN schools reckoned that many of these black students had been misclassified. As Sally Tomlinson has remarked, these teachers believed that 'a misplacement was four times more likely in the case of immigrant children and that the methods and processes of attainment were the major reasons for this misplacement' (1981b, p.75).

Disquiet amongst the black communities about the maltreatment of their children by Local Education Authorities was by no means confined to Inner London. In the nearby Outer London Borough of Haringey, for instance, members of the North London West Indian Association (NLWIA) also expressed concern about the lack of educational progress by their children. There, according to Leila Hassan and Barbara Beese, the proportion of Afro-Caribbean students in local ESN schools was 'a staggering 70 per cent' in 1965–66 (1982, p.25). By May 1971 this controversy attracted greater attention when a modified version of Bernard Coard's talk to the Caribbean Education Association was published. Ten thousand copies of the pamphlet, How the West Indian Child is Made Educationally Subnormal in the British School System, were sold and this helped to crystallize the ESN issue as a focal point for discussion and dispute within and outside the black communities of London. So how did the ILEA administrators and politicians respond to this rising tide of discontent?

To all intents and purposes they did nothing publicly to assuage these anxieties and protests. Instead, as Briault's 1973 document testifies, the Authority retained a commitment to a community-oriented education service in which social disadvantage and not racism was taken as the predicate for policy intervention and resource allocation. The interpretation of data from the R and S group's longitudinal literacy survey did little to disturb Briault's conviction that any (educational) problems experienced by black students in school derived largely from their newness in the UK educational system. Little's conclusion that 'length of education in the United Kingdom appears to be a more important factor determining primary school perform ance than length of residence or being born in this country' paralleled Briault's diagnosis exactly (1975, p.67). Many in the Authority continued to believe that it was a transient problem which would diminish with the passage of time.

But as we indicated in the previous chapter an emphasis on alienation and the increasing 'criminalisation' of black youth during the 1970s rendered such a view at best optimistic, even complacent. Governmental concern over black youths in both school and post-school settings escalated into a 'moral panic' in this period (Hall, et al, 1978) and through mediating bodies such as the DES, Community Relations Commission (CRC) and parliamentary Select Committees, central government urged the education system into adopting immediate ameliorative action. In 1974 the CRC report, Unemployment and Homelessness, noted how the 'vital role of education was universally acknowledged by the experts' in curbing the drift of black youth into criminal activities. It insisted that the educational system was 'not providing a substantial section of young people and particularly of young black people with qualifications adequate to meet either their own expectations or the actual demands of adult life'. According to the CRC the 'blame' could be laid fairly and squarely with the schools, many of which,

> ... have not adjusted to the needs of West Indian pupils, but were carrying on as if nothing had changed from when all pupils were indigenous and white (1974, p.27).

Nor had the educational problems experienced by black youth diminished with the rapidity or inevitability which Briault and others had anticipated. Data generated by the later phases of the ILEA's longitudinal survey into reading attainment showed that the problems were not ephemeral. On the contrary, they showed that a process of attrition was in operation; compared to any other specified group in the survey - 'immigrant' or 'non-immigrant', white or black - the educational performance of students of Afro-Caribbean origin deteriorated most dramatically as they progressed through their primary and secondary school careers. Significantly, this evidence was presented to the new Education Officer in early 1977 and was referred to soon after in one of his preliminary reports on multiethnic education. Four years later the research results were released for public scrutiny. In summary form they showed:

(i)   West Indian or black British reading attainment was low at the age of 8 years old and by school-leaving age was relatively lower. Even when account was taken of initial i.e. 8 year old reading ability there remained an unexplained difference between the black and white British group at 15 years.

(ii)   Full education in this country had a marginal impact on black British attainment. The average West Indian school leaver, fully educated, probably born in this country, had a reading level some 3 points higher than the black British who first started school at the junior stage but some 11 points lower than the indigenous school-leaver.

(iii)   Social deprivation (in so far as it was measured in the ILEA Literacy Survey) together with restricted education and attendance at an EPA school probably accounts for about half the difference between the scores of the indigenous and the Black British (Mabey, 1981).

Although the research team had not set out to explicate the possible causes of these discrepancies in relative attainment levels, the importance of 'teacher attitudes and expectations' on black performance was heavily stressed in the report. Having rejected the social deprivation theory as an all-embracing explanation of differences and in the context of a total disavowal of geneticist interpretations, these data were, to say the least, indicative of debilitating influences and processes within the school - influences and processes which were suggestive of racism. What is more the findings vindicated the decision of an increasing number of black parents and community groups in Inner London (and elsewhere) to send their children to black supplementary schools and provide them with the skills denied to them in formal, mainstream educational institutions. Although the attraction of supplementary schools was by no means unique to the Afro-Caribbean communities, nor even a new development within those communities, there was, perhaps, an extra urgency and perceived necessity. As Nel Clark, founder of the Dachwyng Saturday School in South London, has put it: 'A community cannot be passive and allow a racist education system to disadvantage our children. We need to do something' (1982, p.123). The refusal of the Race Relations Board in 1970 to designate the placement of Afro-Caribbean students in ESN schools as 'an unlawful act', the trend towards the categorisation of these students as 'underachievers' and uneducable and the subsequent drift of disillusioned school-leavers and truants into confrontations with the police ensured that the growth of black supplementary schools would gain momentum in the mid-late 1970s.

It seems to us that the ILEA's initiatives in multicultural education from 1977 can only be fully appreciated and understood in the broader historical and political context which we have sketched out here. The move towards separatism, precipitated not so much by a desire to rekindle ethnic identity and cultural pride but as an effort to ensure that black youths were not additionally disadvantaged by a lack of qualifications in their search for a job, challenged the credibility and stability of Inner London's educational provision and the Authority's responsibility under the 1944 Education Act to provide a common and inclusive education for all students. Perhaps the ILEA could also be accused of precipitating rather than averting the incipient 'racial crisis' forewarned in central government reports. By providing what, on the face of it, was an inappropriate educational experience for its Afro-Caribbean students the ILEA education service not only highlighted the anxieties and disquiet of the black communities but also allowed a large mass of relatively poorly qualified and frustrated students on to the streets who felt that they had been discriminated against during their school lives. In this scenario, the role of the ILEA's Education Officer and his colleagues was clear. Their visit to New York city in 1976 had highlighted the likely social and political implications of unrest engendered by the reactions of frustrated and angry school students (manifested in the forms of indiscipline and truancy rates) and their older, unemployed counterparts. The imperative, therefore, was to ensure that such occurrences did not reach parallel heights in Inner London.

The ILEA's policy initiative, then, was essentially reactive; it did not derive from pedagogical foresight but was impelled by broader and more immediate political and social considerations. As the Education Officer admitted, the notion of assimilation which, until then, had prevailed within the education system remained 'attractive (and) contains much that is valuable'; it was, therefore, 'to be modified only with great reluctance'. The stability of the ILEA's system depended, however, on a reformulated approach and the eventual policy document, Multi-ethnic Education, which was published in November 1977 was designed to establish a new set of ground rules based on an effort to 'reconcile the opposed notions of assimilation and separatism'. It began by declaring a set of principles which were, ostensibly, universalistic in thrust:

> ... the essential duty of the Authority continues to be to ensure that all people within its area benefit from the widest possible range of educational opportunities that can be provided. Unequivocally the commitment is to all. Just as there must be no second class citizens, so there must be no second class educational opportunities (1977, p.1. para 1).

The following paragraph, however, disconfirmed this commitment and revealed that the Authority's main cause for concern was with students of Afro-Caribbean origin. In the context of the specific behavioural and academic problems associated with these students in Inner London schools how else could this paragraph be interpreted?

> The Authority has done much to meet the needs of its changing population but despite these efforts and the individual successes achieved, there is some evidence that disproportionate numbers of people from ethnic minority groups are low achievers in terms of educational standards, have low expectations and aspirations, and lack confidence in the education system which itself appears not to take advantage of the vitality and richness to be derived from a multi-cultural society (1977, p.1. para 2).

The type of provisions recommended in the policy also suggested that the ILEA's avowed commitment to meet the needs of the 'wide range of minority ethnic groups' was more apparent than real. With the exception of language provision for non-English speaking students in Authority schools, the educational needs of these students were largely neglected. Even students of Turkish-Cypriot origin whose reading attainment levels also deteriorated inexorably as they passed through their primary and secondary schools (according to the ILEA literacy survey) failed to attract the attention of the policy-makers. Such a restricted focus is only explicable in terms of our earlier analysis, an argument endorsed by the insistence in the policy that those in the Authority were determined to ensure that 'within a society, that is cohesive not uniform, cultures are respected, differences recognized and individual identities are secure' (1977, p.4. para 1. Emphasis added). As we have already said, the problems experienced by students of Afro-Caribbean origin and the anxiety this stimulated constituted the greatest threat to the ideal of social cohesion.

Our analysis suggests that the label, 'Benevolent Multiculturalism' may be applied legitimately to the initiatives taken by the ILEA in the 1970s. The absence of any explicit reference to racism and its relationship to the apprehensions of the black communities concerning the education of their children reinforces this argument. The policy quite clearly addressed racial matters in so far as it was precipitated by and directed to Afro-Caribbean students, first and foremost. But it barely touched the issue of racism. Instead, by embedding the policy in a conceptual framework informed by cultural pluralism it distracted attention away from racism within the education sustem. Without wishing to promote a conspiratorial view of these developments it is important, nevertheless, to account for what was, in essence, a political manoeuvre.

If we were to believe uncritically the views of those involved in drafting the policy then two reasons for the omission of an antiracist commitment would be accepted. First, in the presence of the 1976 Race Relations Act, the ILEA did not need to declare publicly its commitment to antiracist principles; in the words of one elected member: 'we regarded it as unnecessary to say that we were in favour of not breaking the law'. Second, according to one ILEA inspector: 'if you remember back to 1977 people weren't talking about racism, it wasn't generally being discussed'. Both these explanations fly in the face of the facts, however. The black communities in Inner London prioritised an antiracist commitment in their list of demands to the LEA. And it was through the machinery of the ILEA/CRC consultative committees that this issue was conveyed to the Authority. In December 1976, for example, a member of a local Community Relations Council put it to the ILEA/CRC committee that racialism was on the rise and that it was incumbent on 'the education service to play a vital part in reversing this development'. The failure of ILEA policy-makers to respond to this and related demands led to widespread disenchantment amongst the local black communities, a member of which expressed it like this: 'The policy has gone right the way down the wrong alley and the main reason is because people didn't recognise racism in an institutional sense as something that would affect even the most well-meaning efforts'.

The deliberate avoidance of preparing an antiracist commitment was based partly on political pragmatism. In the ILEA, as well as other LEAs, the determination to achieve bi-partisan support for multicultural/ethnic education policies meant that contentious issues, such as racism, were kept off the agenda. The aim in the ILEA, according to one elected member, was to 'get everybody behind' the policy; 'the policy wasn't challenged seriously because it was prepared with such a lot of care'. From this vantage point we can also understand why the mother tongue issue was avoided in the document. In stark contrast to the principle of cultural diversity – which could easily be accomodated within the Authority's commitment to equality of opportunity – mother tongue provision 'smacked of separatism' and was liable to arouse opposition. 'Social cohesion' to which the policy explicitly was geared could not be realised, or so it seemed, if the separatist movement within the black communities was allowed to continue unchecked. By promoting cultural pluralism, ILEA policy-makers hoped to assuage the anxieties of the black communities and restore their confidence in a system which had been seen to fail their children. Put in the most simple terms, the political goal of social cohesion was translated into the educational goal of securing equality of opportunity for all students in Inner London schools.

MANCHESTER: THE 'CULTURAL UNDERSTANDING' APPROACH:

In Manchester, racial matters in education have assumed less conflictual significance than, say, in the ILEA (Rex, Troyna and Naguib, 1983). Neither the apparent trend towards black 'educational underachievement' nor the communities' moves towards separatism constituted such a severe or obvious threat to the structure or credibility of Manchester's mainstream education provision. This is not to suggest that the educational performance of black students was necessarily on a par with their white colleagues; rather, in the absence of any statistical analysis of performance along ethnic lines nobody was sure of the pattern. At least, that is, until 1980 when Geoffrey Driver's study, Beyond Underachievement was published. Although he did not focus exclusively on the relative performance levels of black and white students in Manchester one of the sample schools included in the survey was a local inner-city, multiethnic school. And Driver's interpretation of his data gave local officers no cause for concern over the performance of black students in public examinations.

As we suggested earlier in the chapter, Manchester's policy statement was stimulated by other concerns and rationalised largely in terms of what Gibson has typified as the 'cultural understanding' approach to multicultural education. According to Gibson:

> The key assumptions underlying this approach are that schools should be oriented toward the cultural enrichment of all students, that multicultural education programs will provide such enrichment by fostering understanding and acceptance of cultural differences, and that these programs will in turn decrease racism and prejudice and increase social justice (1976, p.9).

In short, policy-makers in Manchester were keen to promote a universalistic programme of reforms rather than confining their attention and provisions to black students. The title of their policy, Education for a Multicultural Society, the rationale for its formulation and the organisational and administrative arrangements which stemmed from it give some flavour of the orientation of Manchester's approach. Before elaborating this argument it is useful to present an outline of the LEA's responses to the presence of black students in its schools in the 1960s and 1970s.

Like London, the city of Manchester has experienced a long history of white and black migrant settlement. According to the 1971 census, the New Commonwealth-born (i.e. black) population resident in the city numbered 17,290 and consisted mainly of migrants who had arrived from the Caribbean, especially Jamaica, and South Asia. By 1978, this number had increased to over 50,000 but remained confined mainly to what a former Chief Education Officer (CEO) classified as 'inner-city areas with housing and amenity problems (which) have been designated educational priority areas' (1974, p.1).

The upward trend in the local black population was naturally reflected in city schools. In 1970 black students had comprised 5.7 per cent of the total schools' population; by 1973 the proportion had risen to 6.3 per cent and in 1978 they constituted 11 per cent. Given the skewed distribution of the residential pattern of the local black communities it was not surprising that their children were to be found in a relatively small handful of schools. In 1978, 55 schools (out of the then total of 312) comprised 10 per cent or more black students and 45 schools included 33 per cent and above on their rolls.

Against this background, LEA administrators saw little need to depart from what had been their traditional mode of response to white migrant children. They therefore eschewed the idea of dispersal and rejected proposals to establish reception centres for (black) non-English speaking students. The CEO characterised the approach in the following terms:

> The traditional view is that Manchester has always been a welcoming community to all manner of people from all manner of cultures. It has a proud record of taking in many of the Eastern European refugees from oppression, particularly Jews. It has a very proud Ukranian community and some Polish people. So there is no difference in the measures needed and the response needed for the settling of those who have come from Asia and the West Indies. They will be welcomed for what they are; there is no need to do anything special for them...

> The Education Committee and Officers believed that the right thing was to go to the school appropriate to where you lived and if that resulted in a concentration of children which were assumed to present a problem to this school, to tackle them there with resources into the school but not to put them in specific reception centres.

In certain ways then, the local policy response departed from centrally-prescribed advice; in ideological terms, however, the thrust remained assimilationist and considerable emphasis was placed on language provision. A slightly more subtle analysis reveals that policy responses in the early 1970s were predicated on a compensatory education model. The significant presence of black students in any one school denoted a need to allocate that school additional financial resources; schools which comprised a relatively large proportion of Blacks were also allowed generous teacher-pupil ratios. This broadly-based approach was also reflected in the allocation of responsibilities in the LEA's administration. The Curriculum Development Leader, for instance, who had responsibility for race-related matters, worked under the direction of the Senior Stage Inspector for Special

Education. And when in 1976 the Education Committee appointed an Inspector for Special Education, the successful candidate realised only after he had been appointed that he would be responsible for racial matters even though, on his own admission, he was not 'competent to take on the issue'. In sum then, the tendency in this period was to subsume the matter under the heading of disadvantage and deprivation and to equate the needs of black students with those of their white, working class classmates.

Margaret Gibson informs us that the 'cultural understanding' approach emerged in the United States mainly through the efforts of various ethnic groups determined to ensure that schools 'became more sensitive to cultural differences and modify school curricula to reflect more accurately their concerns' (1975, p.9). There are certainly parallels here with the demands expressed by the black communities in Manchester at this time. On the one hand voluntary black groups such as the West Indian Organisations Co-ordinating Committee (WICC), which had been set up in the city in the late 1960s, voiced their concern at the way the LEA routinely equated black and white working class needs. The conflation of these needs, according to one spokesperson of WICC, was illusory 'because over and above the disadvantages of the working class are the problems of racism and discrimination'. The specificity of racial disadvantage, in other words, was ignored consistently by the Authority. Following this line of argument, WICC demanded greater exploitation of Section 11 monies and the deployment of staff funded from this source into ethnically-mixed schools. Other voluntary groups, however, dissented from this particularistic approach and said that a multicultural education policy could only be effective if it was geared towards the elimination of racist attitudes and practices and the abolition of the monocultural and ethnocentric orientation of the curriculum. In other words, efforts should be directed towards the cultures and assumptions of the white communities.

To all intents and purposes these demands fell on deaf ears until 1977-78 when events in Manchester and elsewhere stirred policy-makers into action. What first caught their eye was the apparent electoral growth of the National Front and its increased agitational activities, including marches in Manchester in October 1977. Nor did the launching of the party's youth wing, Young National Front, in January 1978 go unnoticed. Soon after came Mrs Thatcher's infamous claim on World in Action (January 1978) that the country was being 'swamped' by black immigrants. In all, these developments played a significant role in precipitating a re-appraisal and subsequent re-orientation of the Authority's conception of and policy response to race-related issues. These wider social and political issues were heavily stressed by the CEO in his report to the Policy and Estimates Sub-Committee in March 1978. As he admitted, the LEA was committed to a critical review of existing policy and provision for a number of reasons. Nevertheless, at least part of the pressure to do this,

... at the moment is undoubtedly coming from the recent revival of activity by the National Front. Its importance is underlined by the national political debate about immigration policies. To date Manchester schools have reported only one incident involving National Front activities close to school entrances and the Committee made public immediately their strong support for those teachers who firmly resisted attempts to distribute literature to pupils on school property. No other reports of incidents have been received from schools. A number of organisations have asked that the Education Committee should clearly state their opposition to any attempts by the National Front to infiltrate schools. It has to be acknowledged that the nature of parts of the current national debate and events beyond the scope of the education service are not at present helping schools to evolve good multicultural teaching.

Two very important issues are encapsulated here. First, the recognition that any initiative in education along multicultural lines could be impaired, if not entirely vitiated by wider social and political realities. Paraphrasing the ILEA approach for the moment, we could say that while Manchester's CEO was determined not to provide 'second class educational opportunities', nevertheless he acknowledged that 'parts of the national debate and events beyond the scope of the education service' might still endorse the reality of 'second class citizenship'. In short, the power of education was heavily circumscribed. Second, the CEO admitted to the debilitating influence of racism through the resurgence of NF activity. Of course, this was only a limited concern with racism, but it was a concern nevertheless.

The main purpose of the 1978 report was to set in motion a process of consultation between the LEA, local black community groups and individual schools which would provide the direction and thrust of a reconstituted policy. But it was the LEA policy-makers who set the agenda for discussion and this included: 'inadvertent discrimination'; suitability of attainment tests; the treatment of West Indian students; multicultural education in "all white" schools and, ground rules for the appointment and deployment of Section 11 staff. It was hoped that the results of consultation around these themes would allow the LEA to put some flesh on its commitment 'to ensure the continued development of multicultural education throughout the city'; a commitment spelt out in the 1978 document by the chairperson of the Education Committee.

In the event, the consultative procedure took two years to complete and it was not until June 1980 that the CEO was able to present his 'multicultural package' of three documents to the Education Committee. The first two documents simply outlined existing provision in Manchester and described the consultative exercise. The third report, however, included recommendations for action and a reformulated approach based on a 'clear and unequivocal' commitment to the principles of cultural pluralism. It encouraged all schools in the Authority to 'adopt a pluralist approach and to actively seek ways to use the minority cultures of our community'; the intended outcome of such a policy? The development of 'good relations on the basis of mutual respect for different cultures'. In this scenario, which exemplified all the constituent elements of Gibson's 'cultural understanding' approach, the establishment of an Ethnic Studies Unit was assigned a major role. The purpose of the Unit was 'to develop a source of expertise on the cultures of the main minority groups'. Here, then, we see a fundamental shift in emphasis from the principles addressed in 1978. Then, the security of black students was seen to be threatened by racism and what was implied was an antiracist stance by the LEA and its schools. By 1980, however, concern had shifted to ignorance about 'cultural minorities' as the main stumbling block to 'good relations'. The strategy, then, was to provide all students with more information and insight into these cultures in the expectation that tension and hostility would then be magically undercut. Racism was not mentioned in the 1980 report; it had been replaced by what we characterised earlier as part of the conventional wisdom of multicultural education; namely, 'that learning about other cultures will reduce children's (and adult) prejudice and discrimination towards those from different cultural and ethnic backgrounds' (Bullivant, 1981, p.236). This approach was condemned fundamentally by a member of the local Black Parents Association:

> It might make some people happier; it might give some teachers a sense of being liberal and genuinely concerned about making English education less ethnocentric. It does not seek to address the political culture of the inner city, the local multiracial community. It's no different to central government giving bursaries for social workers to go on safari trips to Trinidad etc.. It begins to deal with culture and aspects of ethnic life without looking at where education fits in with the class set up.

Put another way, the line of reasoning enshrined in Manchester's policy assumed a direct and causal link between life styles and life chances. But it failed to interrogate those wider social and structural realities which circumscribe the life opportunities of black students and which constitute the main block to the realisation of equality of opportunity in a racially-stratified society. Nor, from a more academic point of view, is there much evidence to support the efficacy of the cultural understanding approach. In fact, the research evidence universally contradicts this optimistic assumption if the studies cited by Gibson (1976) and Bullivant (1981), amongst others, are to be believed. In the words of Chris Mullard (1982) they are based on a 'wishful thinking' approach to social change.

MULTICULTURAL EDUCATION IN ACTION

We have been concerned in this chapter with the ways in which two pioneering LEAs set about framing multicultural education policies in the late 1970s. As we have seen, the policies were logical enactments of theories about multiculturalism which were stimulated by specific local concerns. In consequence, they were based on different key assumptions, developed along different trajectories and were geared to different target populations. But there are also commonalities in these approaches. First, both were reactive rather than proactive moves - educational responses to political issues which challenged the stability and credibility of the local education systems. Second, the reformulated approaches were aimed at reducing conflict and minimising tension between groups designated as racially different. The aim in both instances was to provide harmony and cohesion through the intervention of educationally-based reforms. Third, the focus was on the ethnic and cultural backgrounds and life styles of black students rather than the wider political culture in which the life chances of these students were to be determined. The 3Ss interpretation of cultural pluralism subordinated political realities to cultural artefacts. In both Inner London and Manchester the 3Ss was seen to constitute a reformist strategy which would act sufficiently as a panacea for more fundamental social injustices. Finally, both policies were deracialised in their formulation and enactment. Neither LEA recognised the extent to which their provision operated along lines which to a greater or lesser degree discriminated against black students. Political exigencies clearly played a part in this process as policy-makers in Inner London and Manchester were concerned, almost above all else, that their policies should attract bipartisan support. The avoidance of contentious issues was apparently critical in this process. As a result, however, both policies were vulnerable to the sorts of criticisms levelled at the multicultural model by groups such as the Institute of Race Relations; namely, that it prescribes reforms which 'tinker with educational techniques and methods and leaves unaltered the racist fabric of the educational system' (1980, p.82). As we shall soon see the emergence of so-called antiracist education policies in a small handful of LEAs, while eschewing the cultural pluralist paradigm enshrined in the ILEA and Manchester policies, nevertheless also fail to address this matter adequately.

FOOTNOTES

1. The empirical data used to illustrate our arguments in these two case studies derive from research carried out by Troyna in Inner London and Manchester. It draws heavily on his interviews with past and present officers, elected members, advisory teachers and inspectors and members of black community groups in the two cities. A more detailed version of how and why these LEAs formulated policies on multicultural education can be found in chapters 2 and 3 of Rex, Troyna and Naguib (1983) and in Troyna (1984c).

Chapter Three

INSTITUTIONAL RACISM: THE RACIALISATION OF POLITICAL
AND EDUCATIONAL ISSUES

An analysis of shifts in educational policies related to 'race' needs to
be set in the wider context of economic changes and with regard to
the development of the state's policies on immigration and law and
order. It also has to take account of teachers' perceptions of their
everyday problems of the organisation of education and of
ideologically acceptable modes of understanding educational issues.
In short, the ways in which professional interpretations of the context
and creation of educational problems are generated. We have
outlined the deracialisation of educational discourse from the 1960s
onwards as the result of the complex, sometimes contradictory
relationships between these different levels of the social formation.
One of our major points was that the prevalence of deracialised
rhetorical forms in this period does not suggest that racial issues were
unimportant or that racial inequalities were being mitigated.

Within this overall unity of national developments and concerns
there was clearly room for local variations and the specific influences
of local pressures and circumstances. We pointed to some of these in
chapter 2 and demonstrated how the selection and designation of
certain issues and themes as legitimate areas of concern necessarily
kept others off the official policy agenda. Now we want to focus on
the most important of these alternatives; namely, the understanding
of social processes in racialised terms. (As we wrote in our
introduction, we use this term in the manner suggested by Reeves
(1983) that is, to denote 'a growing awareness of, and indignation at,
racial injustice'). Naturally, during the period of deracialisation many
Blacks and white antiracists campaigned for the recognition of racism
as a negative influence in the educational system and for policy-
makers to engage directly and unequivocally with this issue. But their
demands tended to go unheeded. In contrast, the current use of
'Blacks' as a descriptive category in preference to the terms,
'immigrant' or 'ethnic minorities' gives some flavour of the growing
political centrality of colour in educational policy and discourse. In
this and following chapters we want to specify the reasons for both
the trend toward (benign) racialisation and the particular forms in
which this has been embodied in the educational context.

MULTICULTURAL V ANTIRACIST EDUCATIONISTS:

Even a cursory perusal of contemporary education policy documents would show that racism and institutional racism constitute increasingly significant descriptive and explanatory concepts. From this vantage point educationists hope to reveal the nature of racial inequalities, their reproduction, and the facilitating role of schools in this process. This has led ultimately to policy changes summarised as antiracist. Because of this trend it seems to us important that we should consider in some detail the origins and various uses of the terms racism and institutional racism. We can then look at the relationship between the diagnosis of issues and the proposed remedies. But let us begin by establishing the truth of our claim that antiracism and institutional racism are the key concepts in this racialisation process.

Tuku Mukherjee has argued that: 'if we accept that at the centre of the conflict lies the issue of race and racism, then the only viable and meaningful model to work from in education is the antiracist model' (1983). The Institute of Race Relations (IRR) argued along the same lines in its evidence to the Rampton Committee. Members of the IRR called for a radical shift in the understanding of educational issues; they maintained that it would 'involve an honest appraisal of institutional racism within the education system as a whole, in which large numbers of children are consigned to ESN and "sink" schools, and streamed out of exam entry classes or directed away from academic subjects to craft and manual subjects' (1980, p.82). And according to Crispin Jones and Keith Kimberley: 'Schooling is itself an integral part of the operation of institutional racism in society' (1982, p.135). The central role which these writers accord racism and institutional racism is obvious, but it is by no means exceptional. It reflects current emphases in the extant literature which shows not only a dramatic shift in the way educational problems are currently conceived and understood, but also how the new emphases lay claim to superior diagnostic salience. Mukherjee and the others postulate an explanatory framework which is opposed to, rather than a variant on, multiculturalism and the associated range of proposals which we outlined in our previous chapters. Most advocates of antiracist models claim to provide different definitions of educational problems, different explanations of their origins, different policies to remedy these problems and a different analysis of the state's involvement in the creation and resolution of the problems. We are not arguing that all antiracists share a common understanding of racism or of the approaches necessary for attacking its manifestations, however (see Sivanandan, 1985). Our point is that despite important variations within the antiracist framework it constitutes a significant departure from multicultural models. We can highlight this stark contrast by juxtaposing antiracist and multicultural views on a range of concerns.

(a)   definitions of problems

Writers such as Maureen Stone (1981) criticise multiculturalists for defining the educational difficulties stemming from a multiracial society as problems resulting from the presence, per se, of black children.   These include 'underachievement', lack of motivation, indiscipline and alienation, low self-esteem, damaged personal identities and cultural differences. Antiracist theorists, on the other hand, define white racism as the main problem.   This is said to manifest itself in racist ideologies, racialist practices and structural inequalities.   From this perspective then, the alienation of black students, for example, is not pathological but a rational response to racism in the education system.   Amongst others, Dhondy (1982) suggests that alienation can be seen as an affirmation of black pride and resistance.   Antiracists adhere to the view that racism is an integral feature of the education system and that it manifests itself habitually in institutional forms.

(b)   Origins of educational problems

This is another area of disagreement.   At the risk of oversimplification multiculturalist explanations of the educational problems of black students can be categorised in the following ways:

(i)   the relationship between black students and UK society produces lack of self-respect and/or identity problems.

(ii)   the black family (and especially the relationships between parents and children) is not a stable or secure background from which the child will benefit educationally.

(iii)   black cultures are not acknowledged or respected in school settings.

(iv)   disadvantaged or deprived material positions in society militate against learning.

In her criticism of multiculturalism, Stone (1981) has argued that cultural deprivation has been used to account for the black students' allegedly low self-image and that, in consequence, 'underachievement' and/or cultural differences are seen as the basis of educational disadvantage. Jagdish Gundara (1983) makes a similar criticism when he suggests that multiculturalism is embedded in notions of deprivation, disadvantage and underprivilege, all of which legitimise existing power differences.   Antiracist theorists reject summarily explanations built on these grounds.   Their efforts are geared toward analyses of the origin and perpetuation of racism and the production and reproduction of racial inequality.   And institutional racism figures prominently in their explanations.

(c) remedial policies

Policies stem from explanatory frameworks, or should do so in a logical and consistent world. Multiculturalists put forward a range of policies which can be labelled as compensatory - designed to remedy the supposed linguistic, cultural and identity deficits of black students. In this context, the development of a multicultural curriculum to increase students' motivation and commitment to achievements in school, is heavily stressed. It is also hoped that such a curriculum might re-educate white students out of their prejudices. Antiracists, however, press for a very different set of policy changes, ones which are intended to change existing patterns of racial inequality in education by undermining the institutionalisation of racism. In short, the aim is defined in terms of equality of outcomes not equality of access. Richard Hatcher and Jane Shallice (1983) argue that this emphasis on outcomes is necessary because of existing contradictions between equality of opportunity and the 'racial' allocation of achievement; or put differently, between cultural pluralism and actual cultural subordination. Antiracists, therefore, argue for policy initiatives designed to change institutions rather than children. These include the politicisation of the formal curriculum, scrutiny of the 'hidden' curriculum, changes in the way students are assessed and allocated to ability streams and sets, more black staff and better promotion prospects for those already teaching, and the introduction of policies to prevent and punish racist incidents in school. Of these, the formal curriculum has received most attention. As numerous books and pamphlets have indicated, a politicised curriculum would discuss the origins and manifestations of racism and would be directed as much to white as black students.(1) Moreover, special needs would be defined by black groups themselves and special provision would be available as a right of citizenship, not as a compensatory strategy. Seen in this light, mother tongue provision would be seen at least as important as ESL in the formal curriculum.

(d) The hidden agenda of the state

The aims of the state in allowing, supporting, even developing multicultural education policies have been carefully scrutinised and questioned by many observers (see Carby, 1982; Hatcher and Shallice, 1983; Sivanandan, 1984). A number of them have typified this process as the means by which the state can control and contain the resistance of black youth. They suggest that 'underachievement', indiscipline and truancy are signs of a refusal to accept both the legitimacy of the meritocratic system and of individual mobility as a solution to group oppression. Viewed from this perspective, multiculturalism constitutes the state's attempt to maintain social stability and defuse racial conflict rather than a challenge to institutional racism. But policies based on antiracist models of educational change ostensibly eschew this concern with harmony and integration and would not attempt to co-opt black students in order to defuse resistance. Instead, they would link educational issues with wider political strategies. For Mullard (1984) then, antiracism is qualitatively different from multiculturalism in so far as it stems from an entirely different source - blacks rather than (middle class) whites - and is aimed at the goal of racial equality and justice, not harmony and integration. Therefore, the role of the state in the production and reproduction of racism assumes a new and central position in this alternative analysis.

This juxtaposition of multicultural and antiracist perspectives on education indicates their ostensibly distinctive analytical and policy thrusts. We are not arguing that antiracism has ousted entirely multicultural principles and policies however. A brief glance at LEA and school policy statements shows that multiculturalism remains the dominant orthodoxy in these settings. The point we wish to make is that an increasing number of educational institutions have embarked upon a benign racialisation of their policies and some have reformulated their understandings and practices accordingly. It is this process we now wish to subject to detailed scrutiny. Chapters 4, 5 and 6 are concerned with the rise and content of antiracist education policy initiatives. Here we focus upon the intellectual origins and justifications for this form of racialisation process.

While we would agree that antiracist policies represent a significant advance over earlier models and formulations, the indiscriminate use of racism and institutional racism as key explanatory concepts gives us cause for concern. The reasons for our misgivings can best be illustrated through an historical account of the origins of these terms and, in particular, the ways in which academic interpretations of them have influenced subsequent educational and policy discourses in the U.S.A. and U.K.

RACISM AND INSTITUTIONAL RACISM: USE AND ABUSE

The last few years have witnessed heated academic discussions and disputes about the meaning of the term, racism (see, for example, Banton, 1977; Gabriel and Ben-Tovim, 1978; CCCS, 1982; Miles, 1982; Rex, 1982). Nevertheless, all accept that the categorisation of human groups into 'races' has a long history which can be traced back to the sixteenth century and which has subsequently been legitimated by ideologies which have related phenotypical traits to both cultural forms and the evaluation of comparative worth and status. Where these academics disagree, however, is over the precise relationship of these trends to phenomena such as slavery, colonialism, neocolonialism and the changing forms of capitalism and class relations within social formations. We cannot go into this complex debate here, of course (but see Solomos, forthcoming). What is important for our analysis are the ways in which these debates have been answered from within one theoretical framework namely, that which has been signalled by the notion of institutional racism. It is therefore important to look at the origins of this term, its development, theoretically, in both the USA and UK, and finally, its application to educational contexts.

The term, institutional racism, was popularised by Stokely Carmichael and Charles V Hamilton in 1967. It rapidly gained acceptance in the USA as both a descriptive and explanatory concept and was developed by a group of influential theorists (including Baron, 1969; Benokraitis and Feagin, 1974; Blauner, 1972: Jones, 1972, Knowles and Prewitt, 1969 and Wellman, 1977) and educationists, such as Baratz and Baratz, (1970), Katz, (1978) and Spears, (1978).

Carmichael and Hamilton were influential theoreticians of the Black Power movement in the United States and in chapter 1 of their book, Black Power, they developed an analysis of racial inequality and the perpetuation of the ghetto in urban America, as a prelude to a discussion of the political strategies which Blacks could use productively to challenge their racial oppression. It was in this opening chapter that Carmichael and Hamilton contrasted individual with institutional racism: the latter being described as less overt, more subtle and associated with established and respected institutions in society. Importantly, it was the consequences of institutional racism that interested Carmichael and Hamilton more than an analysis of its operation.

But their discussion influenced other writers who proceeded to provide definitions of the term. For James Jones institutional racism referred to 'those established laws, customs and practices which systematically reflect and produce racial inequalities in American society'. He continued: 'if racist consequences accrue to institutional laws, customs or practices the institution is racist whether or not the individuals maintaining those practices have racist intentions' (1972, p.131). Robert Blauner also emphasised unintentional and routine procedures in his analysis, which he termed 'the chains of unwilling actions' (1972, p.188). For him: 'the contingencies of social position, of institutional role are more significant than an individual attitude or person in determining those actions and decisions that make a difference with respect of racial realities' (1972, p.188). Nijole Benokraitis and Joe Feagin were critical of these and other definitions and descriptions however, and provided a more detailed exposition of the term:

Institutional racism refers to the structure of inequality (1) reflected in the racially based differential allocation of status, privileges and material rewards in numerous institutional sectors; and (2) shaped by the historically precipitated and currently persisting processes of subordination whose mechanisms primarily involve the imposition of conventional norms by often unprejudiced role players in the various institutional sectors, in a way which, though covert and usually unintentional, produces racially relevant consequences (1974, pp.23-24).

A number of significant points emerge from these initial uses of the term. First all the analysts stressed the significance of racist ideologies in initiating, sustaining and justifying racial inequalities and oppression. But as the term, racism, is used by Carmichael and Hamilton and others, it does not denote an ideology. Rather, it refers to a range of other processes. These include decisions and policies which have been designed to subordinate and/or control blacks; active and pervasive anti-black attitudes, and attitudes which are said to result in racial inequalities. Either racism and institutional racism were often used interchangeably, or institutional racism was subsumed within the term, racism, precisely because of the latter's breadth of meaning. Blauner, at least, was aware of the theoretical muddle which derived from the indiscriminate and all-embracing use of the term and insisted that: 'if racism is to be a useful concept for understanding oppression and social change in America, it cannot be used as a magical catchphrase to be applied mechanically to every situation without analysing its specifics' (1972, p.259).

The second point which emerges from these writings is that institutional racism was not used as an explanatory concept in it own right. It was a member of a group of concepts which, together, were invoked to explain racial oppression. Of the others, internal colonialism had the most powerful resonance. Raymond S. Franklin and Solomon Resnick (1973) likened urban ghettos to a neo-colonial situation by describing the ways in which material necessities were imported from outside, profits were exported, low paid labour was exported and, foreign aid was received in the form of welfare. Blauner (1972) carried this analogy further. He argued that entry into the ghetto was forced and involuntary. It resulted from conquest and slavery and the colonisers destroyed or transformed indigenous values and life styles. The colonised were administered by representatives of the dominant group who used racism as their principal justification for social domination. Blauner argued that Blacks in the USA occupied a unique social and political role, for although white ethnics in America might be exploited they were not colonised.

The third significant point is that institutional racism was used to describe how the interrelationships between different institutions reinforced racial inequality. This aspect of the term was underlined, especially, by Carmichael and Hamilton: 'The core problem within the ghetto is the vicious circle created by lack of decent housing, decent jobs and adequate education..... the pervasive cyclic implication of institutional racism' (1967, p.156).

The fourth distinguishing characteristic of this approach is the emphasis placed upon the benefits which whites derive from racism and its institutionalisation. As David Wellman put it, racism constitutes 'culturally sanctioned beliefs which, regardless of intentions, defend the advantages of the whites' (1977, p.xviii).

It is precisely the location of power in the hands of the white population which made institutional racism so difficult to dismantle, according to Carmichael and Hamilton. However, the question of which white groups gained most from its presence in the social structure remained an issue for contention. Harold Baron (1969) believed that a multitude of small white groups gained economically and psychologically. Blauner tended to agree. For him, skin colour served 'as a visible badge of group membership that facilitates the blockage of mobility' and prevented the development of citizenship which might integrate the working class (1972, p.37). Following this line of argument, white workers would be aware that they would be disadvantaged if racial inequalities were eliminated. This insistence that almost all Whites, irrespective of class position, benefit from racism is quite different from Cox's arguments. He maintained that it was the members of the capitalist ruling class who benefit most from the perpetuation of racism (1970).

Finally, the emergence of racism as a central analytical concept had important implications for the nature of political strategies. Manning Marable (1984), for instance, has documented the forms of political and cultural nationalism which followed directly and logically from the centralisation of racism as a determinant of life chances. Similarly, Robert Allen (1969) has argued that cultural nationalists in the 1960s emphasised the centrality and autonomy of racism at the expense of a wider understanding of exploitation. The result: the development of struggles for national liberation rather than the initiation of socialist struggles which would have necessitated class alliances across ethnic lines.

This summary of how racism and institutional racism gained credence as explanatory terms in the USA, the nature of their meanings, and of the political strategies which stemmed from their use provides a starting point for an analysis of how those in the UK engaged with these terms. As we shall see there are many similarities.

Derek Humphrey and Gus John were the first writers to popularise the concept, institutional racism, on this side of the Atlantic. Roughly a decade and a half after Carmichael and Hamilton had introduced the term in the USA, Humphrey and John described vividly in their book, Because They're Black, the appalling treatment received by black citizens in the UK. They insisted that this treatment did not derive, purely and simply, from individual discriminatory acts against Blacks but that it had a more subtle, insidious origin and form; that is, racism was institutionalised in Britain. They did not develop a theoretical exposition of the concept but offered, instead, a descriptive definition of its workings: 'Institutional racism - manipulating the bureaucratic system to outflank the unwanted - may not be as rampant in Britain as in America, but it appears vividly among planning and housing regulations' (1971, p.112), as well as within the educational system.

Two years later, Ann Dummett's book, A Portrait of English Racism, provided substantial evidence of the pervasive and determining impact of racism on the lives of black citizens in the UK. Along with Humphrey and John she found the term, institutional racism, eminently serviceable in the context of her account. Thus in a racist society such as Britain there are 'institutions which effectively maintain inequality between members of different groups in such a way that open doctrine is unnecessary, or, where it occurs, superfluous. Racist institutions, even if operated partly by individuals who are not themselves racist in their beliefs, still have the effect of making and perpetuating inequalities' (1973, p.131). The origins of institutional racism, according to Sheila Allen (1973), could be found in the relationships between immigrant and indigenous people,

51

between metropolitan and colonial societies and in the development of the ideology of racism. In this analysis greater emphasis was placed on the consequences of these factors than on the intentions of individuals or particular groups of people. Arguably, the most detailed and insightful exposition of the term has been provided by Steve Fenton in his short article for New Community in 1982. He has suggested that institutional racism is manifest in social structures in which:

> (a) Racism is not only to be found in ideal constructs but in regular practices, rules and the enduring features of society. (b) Racism as a belief or attitude is somehow masked but is nonetheless structurally evident in practice. (c) It may even be conceded that racist attitudes are absent but the structural correlates - inequality, disadvantage and subordination - are still fashioned along racial lines (1982, p.59).

Now although we have only mentioned a few of the many definitions and expositions of the term which have been provided by social scientists and other analysts in the UK since the early 1970s we suggest that they are, to a greater or lesser extent, representative. So how do they compare with their American counterparts? To begin with, there is the same emphasis upon consequences rather than intentional action. Similarly, it is generally agreed that institutional racism connotes something beyond occasional or individual discrimination against Blacks. Racism is seen to extend beyond ideal constructs and embraces practices and structures. In both the USA and UK there is also continuing uncertainty about whether a doctrine of racism is evident, masked or absent. But what is especially important is that institutional racism has now become so popular a concept that it is frequently used in a taken-for-granted way with no accompanying definition or detailed discussion. (see for example, NATFHE, 1984; Newsam, 1984; Willey, 1984). Let us now turn to examples of institutional racism in education where this lack of theoretical sophistication is most marked.

INSTITUTIONAL RACISM IN EDUCATION:

There are, predictably, considerable differences between authors regarding the emphasis placed upon institutional racism as an explanatory variable. For some theorists as we have already seen, institutional racism constitutes not only the most significant but the only way in which an understanding of the way racism operates in the educational system can be fully grasped. For others, such as Gideon Ben-Tovim, it operates not in isolation but in parallel with ideological, cultural, structural and, organisational forms of racism. According to his argument, institutional racism in education refers directly to processes such as the creation of the category, 'immigrant child' which provided the rationale for enforced dispersal; the hidden curriculum of racist values, and the bias of school textbooks. He goes on to say that the consequences of these processes are exemplified by the over-representation of black students in ESN schools and their under-representation in sixth forms and higher education (1978, p.208). Malcolm Saunders also specifies four forms of racism: individual, institutional, cultural and structural. He argues that: 'Institutional racism (now generally called racism) (sic) is expressed covertly. For example, in schools various forms of grouping, such as setting, tracking, streaming and special classes and units may be called institutional racism in so far as they lead to a preponderance of, say, West Indian children in any group of lower attainment' (1982, p.65). Later on in his article, Saunders pinpoints how institutional racism manifests itself in the hidden curriculum. This assumes the form of biases in school organisation: majority group modelling by teachers and peers; discriminatory control techniques; ethnocentric techniques to assess student abilities; and ethnocentric teaching materials. Simply on the basis of the examples suggested by Ben-Tovim and Saunders we can see the delineation of a number of different forms of racial inequality in education (both quantitative and qualitative) and a large number of institutional practices leading to these inequalities. But this is by no means an exhaustive list. For instance, a draft document of the National Association for Teachers in Further and Higher Education (NATFHE) identified institutional racism as 'the discriminatory effects which flow from the rules and procedures of institutions. Such rules and procedures were not designed to discriminate but may militate against the achievement of equality of opportunity' (1984, p.2).(2)   Jane Shallice (1984) has extended the list even further. She suggests that institutional racism accounts for the relatively low number of Blacks recruited into the teaching profession; the concentration of black teachers in the lower echelons of the profession's hierarchy; the neglect of mother tongue provision; the refusal of teachers to take seriously the state's immigration and nationality acts and the general absence of a curriculum to provide all students with an understanding of racism.

The explication of institutionalised racist practices and procedures in education has, in turn, led to a number of policy proposals. A detailed analysis of some of these policies will be provided later. Here, we want to give a flavour of the type and nature of recommendations which antiracist educationists have proposed.

As we noted earlier in this chapter, antiracists have tended to pinpoint the curriculum as the main site for intervention. A curriculum modelled along antiracist lines would, according to its advocates, facilitate a dramatic change in the racial attitudes of staff and students. Nor would these interventionist strategies be confined to the formal curriculum; on the contrary, the hidden curriculum figures prominently in these policy proposals. Amongst many others, Saunders has suggested a strategy for curriculum reform that would be geared toward the removal of institutional racism in schools:

> Since institutional and individual racism and racialism are perceived here as part of the hidden curriculum, they are, by definition, unplanned and often unobtrusive. The basis of their

eradication must be through a process of general sensitisation and the resulting commitment of staff and pupils leading to the scrutiny of traditional patterns of organisation and behaviour, the monitoring of teaching materials and other resources and the increased appointment of staff from ethnic minority groups (1982, p.71)

As Saunders points out, however, the principal target for change in this interventionist strategy is the attitudes and beliefs of staff. Thus he proposes a 'process of general sensitisation' as the starting point for change. In recent years, racism awareness courses for teachers (and others professionally engaged in work with Blacks) have been proposed as the most productive route to attitude change. These courses tend to be influenced by the ideas and strategies pioneered in the USA by Judy Katz (1978) and are predicated on the grounds that by changing the (racial) attitudes of those people who have power in social institutions it will be possible to change institutionalised racialist practices. We want to hold our criticisms of this strategy in abeyance because here it is important to look at the entire range of policy suggestions which emanate from the antiracist perspective.

Briefly put, these crystallize around a concern with the low number of black teachers; the intransigence of examination boards; streaming procedures; physical and verbal racial abuse in school; the level of mother tongue provision and the failure of teachers to demonstrate their commitment to antiracist campaigns beyond the school gates (see ALTARF, 1980; 1984; Hatcher and Shallice, 1983; NUT, 1982).

We can see then that when applied to the educational context the term, institutional racism, incorporates a bewildering array of processes and practices. It is used to signify certain attitudes, beliefs, practices, actions and processes some of which are overt, others covert. Some are said to be intentionally racist in their outcomes, others unintentional. We shall argue in chapters 5 and 6 that this lack of conceptual precision has been transposed directly into formal LEA antiracist policy documents. Before we look at these policies, however, we want to provide a more detailed critique of some theoretical aspects of institutional racism as this will facilitate our later analysis.

INSTITUTIONAL RACISM: A THEORETICAL CRITIQUE:

The initial use of the term by black radicals in the USA stressed two things; the historical institutionalisation of racial inequalities and the perpetuation of these inequalities in contemporary urban settings through the interconnecting relationships of several institutional areas. Since then, however, the term has generally been used to refer to the functions and mechanisms of a single institution, such as a school or factory. In this context, its meaning has become oversimplified; reduced to denoting a direct and causal relationship between one form of inequality (such as black 'educational underachievement') and one institution (e.g. school). So, institutional racism tends to be used, in the first place, in a descriptive manner - to delineate a particular aspect of inequality which is then said to derive from the routine institutional mechanisms operated by people who may or may not be racially prejudiced. (This argument is developed fully by Williams, forthcoming, and Williams and Carter 1985). This ambiguity of meaning has important implications for the application of the term to education and, more specifically, for its legitimacy as a theoretical basis for antiracist education policies.

If institutional racism is defined by its consequences does the presence of any form of racial inequality imply its existence? We have already noted the wide range of educational inequalities referred to in the literature and while we would not question the veracity of the authors' claims we doubt, nevertheless, that these inequalities are all produced and reproduced in the same way. Nor do we believe that the education system is responsible entirely for their creation.

Any measure of racial inequality is comparative and is dependent upon the group(s) with whom the comparison is made. It may be with all Whites, with Whites in a particular geographical area, or social class, or with similar qualifications or job experiences. The point we wish to make is that the nature of the comparisons is frequently hidden or ignored. In analyses of black educational performance, for instance, the nature of comparison has been especially important in the interpretation of raw data. On these grounds, Reeves and Chevannes (1981) criticised the Rampton Committee's failure to take social class into account in its presentation of the relative performance of Afro-Caribbean, South Asian and white indigenous students in public examinations. Inter-group comparisons of academic achievement levels rest on the assumption that like is being compared to like. But as Troyna has argued, this is a spurious assumption when applied to the differential performance of black and white students in UK schools because: 'the relationship of black pupils to society generally, and education in particular, are so profoundly and qualitatively different from those of their white classmates ... that they militate against the use of inter-group comparison as a valid or reliable measurement of performance' (1984a, p.158). A K Spears has gone even further in his critique of comparative academic performance levels: 'any insistence on evaluating the academic accomplishments of blacks - particularly those who have studied in white institutions - in the same way that those of whites are evaluated is another manifestation of institutionalised racism' (1978, p.133 Emphasis added). It seems to us then that empirical studies in education reflect and reinforce the lack of conceptual clarity which is at the very core of the concept, institutional racism.

If the presence of racial inequality alerts us to the existence of institutional racism then, clearly, it is the reproduction of these inequalities by routine institutional procedures which legitimates the use of the concept. Therefore it is necessary that educational discussions are based, at the very least, on the following. First, a clear and unambiguous theoretical outline of the nature of the relationship between institutions. Second, an understanding of the operation and workings of particular institutions. Third, an appreciation of the relationship between individuals who are part of the institution and the structures within which they work. Unfortunately, a grasp of these issues is sadly lacking in the literature.

If institutions are defined as sets of structures and practices which are not reducible to the individuals who staff them, then it is reasonable to expect these structures and practices to be the object of study. What frequently happens, however, is that examples of institutional racism are given from a societal level (for instance, the history of racism) or from an individual level (staff attitudes, for example). In educational studies this often happens in so far as teacher attitudes, expectations and stereotypes are posited as the crucial mechanisms which perpetuate racial inequality. There needs to be a much clearer discussion of the origins of inequalities and institutional procedures which perpetuate these; they cannot be reduced to individual behaviour. Consequently Peter Newsam's claim that: 'A "racist" institution is quite simply one in which discriminatory rules or systems apply and no one has either noticed or tried to remove them' (1984, p.2), seems overtly simplistic.

As we saw earlier, analyses of institutional racism often emphasise non-intentionality or routine institutional procedures. However, individuals' ignorance of the consequences of their actions or their unquestioning acceptance of the rationale for particular procedures are not synonymous with the procedures, per se, having unintended consequences. Often the two are conflated; analytically, however, distinctions need to be made between (a) those activities which are racialist and are supported by racist justifications (such as colour bars); (b) those activities, such as streaming, which are in origin non-racialist and are justified by non-racist ideologies; and (c) those activities which are non-racialist in origin, (such as curriculum decisions, rules concerning uniform and so on) but which can be perpetuated by unadmitted racist justifications. In short, the relationship between racist intent, racialist practices and racist effects (in the form of inequality) are not as clear-cut as many would have us believe. The imperative must be to clarify empirically these relationships if realistic and productive antiracist policies are to be formulated.

We also find in the literature that unintentional racism is used in order to avoid attaching moral blame to individuals (see Rampton, 1981, p.12, for example). Curiously, however, it is invoked simultaneously to justify racism awareness courses where unquestioned assumptions are brought out in the open and moral blame is attached to them! (Gurnah, 1984). This reformist strategy proceeds on the grounds that once individuals have been alerted to their own racism they will consequently wish and be able to alter their own professional practices and the organisation of their schools. In the light of our earlier remarks about the complex relationship between intentions, practices and effects, the assumptive basis of racism awareness courses seems unduly optimistic. Instead, what derives logically from our analysis is the formulation of policies which do not assume either a direct link either between actions and intent or individual conversion with institutional change.

One further point needs to be made in relation to the nature of institutions; that is, the simplistic discussions which currently prevail presume that all institutions are of equal importance and that white individuals are, in general, the source of institutional power. If one accepts the other strand of the antiracist argument namely, that routine institutional procedures constitute an independent entity in the production and confirmation of racial inequalities, then neither the ethnic origin nor the political partialities of individuals operating those procedures are likely to have much impact on this process. Quite clearly, the nature of institutional power and the institutional practices which are said to produce and reproduce racial inequalities require more sensitive and complex attention than they have been accorded so far. It simply cannot be assumed that, prima facie, streaming, teacher stereotyping, the designation of catchment areas, the monocultural curriculum and so on, are causally related to each other or contribute straightforwardly to the generation of racial inequalities. Of course, they are all examples of injustice and should be removed as soon as possible from the educational stage. But their exact relationship to racial inequality can only be theorised not demonstrated empirically at the moment.

EDUCATIONAL AND RACIAL INEQUALITIES:

With one or two conspicuous exceptions discussions of institutional racism in education, and other spheres of social and political life, are based on a taken-for-granted acceptance of the primacy and autonomy of racial identity. As a result, the processes through which racial inequality is perpetuated are neither linked with or understood in conjunction with those that reproduce class and gender inequalities. The absence of these linkages is even more remarkable given the parallels between the earlier educational debates about working class students and those which currently crystallize around the concern with black students. As we demonstrated in chapter 1 explanations for both the 'underachievement' of white working class and black students have tended to be structured in a discourse which emphasises a pathological interpretation of educational failure: concepts such as cultural deprivation, language deficiences and disadvantage have tended to provide the explanatory framework for analysis. Similarly, the aims of educational policies for black students parallel those policies of the 1960s and 1970s which were designed to enhance the educability of white working class students. The comparison between advocacy for community education in the 1970s and antiracist education in the 1980s demonstrates this point exactly. Advocates of these educational reforms emphasise the politicisation of the curriculum through an inclusion of contemporary issues and a focus upon the milieux in which the children live. Both recommend greater parental and community group involvement in the school. There is also agreement about the need for teachers to be re-educated in the expectation that this will encourage them to jettison the monocultural, middle class curriculum and their stereotypical views of working class and black student groups.

We can extend these parallels even further. Certain aspects of the institutionalisation of mass education within capitalist society – the processes of competition, the individualisation of failure, the emphasis upon the cognitive – intellectual definition of achievement – have worked to the detriment of white working class students as well as black students. So when Benokraitis and Feagin argue that credentialism is 'a procedure by which blacks are disqualified from competition because they fail to meet objectively formulated standards' (1974, p.24) they are outlining a process which has historically also impaired the progress and life chances of many white students. Now we are not denying that many of the experiences of black students in schools and colleges are race-specific; the point we want to make is that some are also racial versions of class patterns. Unfortunately, this is often ignored by antiracists.(3) Nor is an understanding of racial inequalities facilitated by the cavalier use of the terms racism and institutional racism. These merely oversimplify the complex relationship between material, ideological and political processes. There is a persistent tendency to portray racial ideologies (stemming from colonialism and imperialism) as directly responsible for negative teacher attitudes, stereotyping, labelling and other processes which, via self-fulfilling prophecies, result in racial inequalities in academic achievement levels. The relationships between these different levels of the social formation are not as clear and unambiguous as this simplistic formulation implies.

It is also necessary to demonstrate empirically the relationships between historically and contemporarily developed ideologies and the commonsense racism of the holders of bureaucratic and professional positions. What in one context is developed as a progressive, challenging ideology may be incorporated into other contexts, reworked, reinterpreted and emerge as a paternalistic, even racist justification for social control measures. Antiracism, as a broad label for a range of ideologies, commonsenses and practices needs to be subject to a similar analysis.

Our final point in this chapter brings us back to the arguments heavily stressed in early American writings, but which seem to have been lost en route to the UK: the interrelationships between different institutions and their impact on the reproduction of racial inequalities. In the specific case of education this is a critical factor. After all, the over-representation of black students in specific school catchment zones, their subsequent presence in schools with relatively poor academic records and, ultimately, their poor performance in public examinations cannot simply be explained in terms of the institutionalised racism of the school. The recruitment of black migrants to low-status, poorly paid jobs and their concentration in particular residential urban areas quite obviously constitute important contributory factors to this trend. It is the confluence of these processes – which are both educational and non-educational - which has resulted in the production of unequal educational outcomes.

Nor can racial inequality in the labour market be mitigated simply through school-based antiracist strategies. Despite what the Rampton Committee implied in its report, equal opportunity for black school-leavers in their search for work would not appear magically through the implementation of policies designed to enhance their academic performance, however successful these might be (1981, p.10). As various researchers have shown, success in educational and occupational spheres is not causal and direct and in the specific case of black youth this 'tightening bond' theory is especially tenuous (Troyna and Smith, 1983; Troyna, 1984b). As our analysis of LEA antiracist policy statements will show, the connecting relationship between different institutions in this context are rarely acknowledged by policy-makers. Such a narrow perspective on, and understanding of, the origins and perpetuation of racial inequalities in contemporary life is likely to create false optimism. While we do not undervalue the need for educational reform in this area it seems to us that the present initiatives simply confirm A. H. Halsey's observation that:

.....there has been a tendency to treat education as the waste paper basket of social policy - a repository for dealing with social problems where solutions are uncertain or where there is a disinclination to wrestle with them seriously. Such problems are prone to be dubbed "educational" and turned over to the schools to solve (1972, p.8).

The veracity of this will be demonstrated in chapter 5. Before then, we want to look at those factors which have led directly or indirectly to the acceptance of an explanatory paradigm summarised by the concept, institutional racism, and to the particular racialised complexion of contemporary educational policy and debate.

FOOTNOTES

1. Examples of antiracist curriculum materials may be found in ALTARF (1984); IRR (1982); Searle (1977) and Straker-Welds (1984).

2. This draft NATFHE document was subjected to much criticism and was revised precisely because of the lack of clarity and political usefulness of its definition of institutional racism.

3. Discussions of assessment procedures in the journal Issues in Race and Education (No. 42, 1984) illustrate this point well.

Chapter Four

THE ORIGINS OF ANTIRACIST EDUCATION POLICIES IN THE UK.

We have argued in previous chapters that education policies and debates, though centrally concerned with issues of colour, and the relationship of colour to social class and citizenship, have been formulated and presented largely in deracialised terms. We suggested that this process enabled racial discrimination and racist ideologies to be perpetuated and racial inequalities to be exacerbated. We then traced the intellectual origins of an alternative analysis, one which has been influential in the trend towards the benign racialisation of educational policy and discourse. In this chapter we will develop this line of argument further and explain how and why these alternative interpretations and related policies concerning black students in the UK education system have gained acceptance by a growing number of academics, professionals and politicians.

In order to accomplish this aim we need to outline two distinctive social processes. The first is an account of the social contexts both in the USA and UK in which particular understandings of racism and institutional racism were generated. We do this because, as we argued in the introduction, we see the social sciences as socially constituted discourses; the emergence of new emphases and concepts reflects the social contexts of their origin and the particular social position of the 'organic intellectuals' who acted as midwives to their birth (Popkewitz, 1984). Following on from this we shall discuss the acceptance and spread of these understandings in terms of particular educational rhetoric and policies summarised as antiracist. We shall focus upon the contexts in which an increasing number of black parents and professionals along with white activists, administrators and politicians have all espoused the antiracist cause.

INSTITUTIONAL RACISM IN CONTEXT: THE USA

We have already noted that the origins of the term, institutional racism, can be found in the USA in the 1960s. At this historical moment certain material, political and ideological contexts came together to provide a setting for a re-interpretation of the nature of racial inequalities. To take the material conditions first: northward migration, urbanisation and proletarianisation of the black population had continued throughout the twentieth century but had accelerated during the 1939-45 war and afterwards. By 1960 the majority of Blacks were city dwelling members of the working class (Sowell, 1981, pp.208-16). This was also a period in which relationships between black and white migrants, and working class blacks and whites in the industrial centres of the North were conditioned and informed fundamentally by skin colour. Marable (1984), for instance, has contended that Blacks and Whites rarely competed for the same jobs precisely because a legalised caste system persisted in the North. Baron (1969) has gone even further in suggesting that the consolidation of a black underclass (dependent on welfare or unskilled jobs for economic survival) coincided with the upward social mobility of many white American in-migrants. But occupational segregation did not operate in isolation; rather, it went hand in hand with residential segregation to the extent that Gerald Grace has contended that: 'the crisis in legitimation in social, economic, racial and political relationships was interpreted in this period as a problem of the cities' (1984, p.6).

The tracing of these broad trends should not blur the point, however, that the 1960s also saw the emergence of a black middle class which contained within its ranks a number of academics who had benefitted from the special university entrance programmes introduced at the beginning of the decade. Of course, black graduates were nothing new in the States. They had been emerging from black colleges and universities, such as Howard University in Washington D.C. ever since the nineteenth century. What was different was the relatively large number of black graduates in the '60s and the nature of their educational careers. A sizeable number had benefitted from the politically-inspired entry programmes which provided access to institutions previously reserved exclusively for white students. It is our contention that the politicisation of these black graduates had an important influence on the way they perceived and interpreted racial inequality in contemporary US society.

The history of the civil rights movement and the varieties of black political groups involved in it is too well known to need repeating here (see Sitkoff, 1981; Marable, 1984). But the shift from demands for the abolition of legal and commercial rules enforcing segregation in the south, to political registration, the rise of Black Power movements and electoral politics in the north is important. The outbreak of the 'burn, baby, burn' riots from 1965 onwards constituted a vivid reminder of racial oppression and signalled the steps which many Blacks were willing to take in resisting racism and associated practices. But it would be wrong to presume that the riots prompted general agreement on the strategies required to ameliorate this condition. In fact, the emergence of class differences within the black population precluded such a consensus. For instance, the black professional middle class tended to support the notion of cultural nationalism and adherence to 'legitimate' modes of political activity as a form of resistance to racism. Black entrepreneurs, on the other hand, saw the consolidation of black capitalism as an answer to the poverty and powerlessness experienced by the mass of black

Americans. Different again were the modes of black nationalism and militancy which were advocated and practiced, from time to time, by some working class Blacks. What is important here, however, is that irrespective of class perspective and the related forms of action they gave rise to, institutional racism, as an all-embracing explanatory concept, could be used by all. Naturally, because it was amenable to various interpretations and purposes it could, and was used selectively; but it was also used within a general understanding of the mechanisms perpetuating racial segregation and inequality. That is to say, a consensus emerged over the following issues. First, it was agreed that the use of statutory and judicial procedures to undercut the nature of racial inequality had been slow and largely ineffective. Second, it was accepted that the actual institutions themselves - the law, political parties, the education system, welfare organisations and so on - were incapable of eradicating their own racialist practices. Third, there was a general rejection of the established explanations for, and conventional strategies to overcome racial inequality. No longer did many people believe that racial oppression would diminish with the passage of time and that a 'melting pot' of cultural diversity would arise, like a phoenix, to take its place. Racial oppression was more firmly engrained in American life and the origins and nature of this, according to the theory of institutional racism, could be found in those institutional processes which created and perpetuated the ghetto - a clear example of black oppression in the States.

As we said earlier, Carmichael and Hamilton played a pioneering role in the advocacy of institutional racism as an explanatory concept. For them, blackness was central to the diagnosis of political ills. It also formed the basis from which the strategies needed to eradicate those ills could be formulated. As they put it in their book: 'before a group can enter open society it must first close its ranks' (1967, p.44). Along with other black activists they pushed for control over the ghetto - particularly its politics, businesses and schools - as a primary objective. In this scenario, institutional racism provided an explanation for their failure to wrest control of these institutions from white dominance.

Nor were radical black academics alone in their fight to establish institutional racism as the explanatory tool for their oppression and inequality. With the growth of Black Power and the outbreak of the 'burn, baby, burn' riots, the issues of 'race' and racism compelled once again the attention of white sociologists in America. And many of them criticised extant theories of racial inequality, especially those theories which reduced its causes exclusively to economic or psychological phenomena. Within sociology, functionalism was being challenged increasingly as the dominant paradigm by interactionist, structuralist and conflict theorists. What is more, the theoretical debates between Weberians and Marxists over the relationships between material inequalities and the formation of ideologies found one expression in an understanding of race relations in terms of institutional racism. In America (and later in the UK) institutional racism assumed great symbolic importance: a signifier of academic and/or political support for certain interpretations of how society operates. In short, it became a means of denoting what one was against as much as what one was for.

The distinctive uses to which institutional racism was put by different groups requires a more detailed analysis than we can provide here. It is clear, nonetheless, that through its emphasis on unintentionality and 'normal institutional procedures' it lifted responsibility and guilt for racial inequality from the shoulders of individuals. In the process its appeal was always likely to be broad. At the same time the benefits which derived from its application were bound to affect some groups more than others. This is a point developed more fully in the American context by Marable (1984). He shows clearly how the black middle class, rather than working class, reaped the benefits from the policy measures initiated in response to a perception of institutional racism. For example, special recruitment policies and forms of positive discrimination were usually developed in particular middle class occupations (teaching, social work, government administration) or in the growth of bureaucracies to organise and allocate special funds and programmes.

From this brief and necessarily sketchy outline we can see how the confluence of economic, political, professional and academic contexts enabled institutional racism to be deployed in a number of different discourses. Moving from the USA we can pinpoint similar processes in the emergence and use of the term in Britain.

INSTITUTIONAL RACISM IN CONTEXT : THE UK

A full and detailed study of the acceptance of racialised theories and concepts would require an outline of the political, economic, academic and bureaucratic contexts within which this occurred. Examples of the transformations of meaning and emphasis which inevitably take place within these different contexts will be outlined in chapters 5 and 6. For the present discussion it is sufficient to argue that the acceptance and use of these concepts in Britain has been influenced in general by the same social forces identified in the American context. Louis Kushnick (1982) argues that there are very close parallels between America in the 1960s and Britain in the 1980s. For example, there has been a growth in black political groups and black voting strength; a rise of a small but influential number of black social scientists; manifestations of frustration and bitterness through demonstrations; the growth of exclusive black cultural groups and the outbreak of 'riots'. The continuing inequality experienced by the black school-leavers, particularly in obtaining jobs or promotion, has been well documented. There is obviously less emphasis in this country upon the ghetto, but black citizens are largely concentrated in inner cities. The passing of immigration legislation designed to keep out Blacks, and governmental emphasis upon immigrants as aliens, or 'the enemy within' has demonstrated the extent of 'official' state racism. At the same time legislation has been introduced in an attempt to limit discrimination and promote racial equality. The 1965, 1968 and 1976 Race Relations Acts are steps in this direction. The 1976 Act included a section on indirect discrimination and another informing local authorities of their duty to prevent discrimination and foster equitable race relations. Both sections are responses to the understanding of unintended or covert racist practices which had been emphasised in the literature on institutional racism.

Academic debates about pluralism, ethnicity and racism have also developed along similar lines to those in the United States, as have social policy debates. The Scarman Report (1981) was very similar in its analysis and recommendations to the McCone Report on the Watts riots. We are also witnessing a gradual but by no means unanimous acceptance in government sponsored reports and legislation that racism plays a part in influencing and circumscribing the life chances of black citizens.[1] In the UK then institutional racism has been used to attack existing theories which blame victims for their own racial oppression. What is more, it has influenced the nature of remedial policies geared to eradicate those practices which allegedly generate and perpetuate racial inequalities. In brief, as we outlined earlier, the acceptance of institutional racism as an explanatory paradigm paves the way for the formulation of policies which identify antiracism as their prime goal. As our focus in this book is on educational policies we need to sharpen our discussion and look closely at why and how antiracism has emerged in recent years as a summarising variable for a range of ameliorative measures related to education.

THE ACCEPTANCE AND LEGITIMATION OF ANTIRACISM

(a) pressure groups:
We argued in chapters 1 and 2 that a number of black groups and individuals had drawn attention to the specific racist nature of their treatment and disadvantage throughout the 1960s and 1970s. We also saw how these appeals were either ignored routinely or reinterpreted within other discourses such as those focussing on 'culture' or disadvantage and deprivation: this is what we called the deracialisation process. But as we can now see, demands along these lines from black parents, community groups and so on, could not be simply wished away. On the contrary, during the 1970s and into the '80s their calls for action have been articulated more vociferously and with greater fervour. The growth of black supplementary and separate schools, the publication of empirical evidence pointing to inequalities in black and white achievement levels, threats of secessions and boycotts, and the forging of alliances between black groups and various local and national antiracist organisations have all precipitated a shift in the thinking and provision of LEAs in different parts of the country. We provided an example of this in chapter 2 in analysing how and why the ILEA changed its public stance in 1977 largely because of fears about fragmentation and secession. Recent events in Berkshire local education authority resulted in similar, arguably more dramatic changes. There, disquiet had been expressed about changes in the school allocation procedures in Reading and their detrimental effect on the opportunities for schooling available to

black students, amongst others. As a direct result of a campaign organised by a coalition of black and white activists, the LEA zoning scheme became the subject of a formal investigation by the CRE. It also led ultimately to the Authority reappraising its established modes of understanding and responding to racial inequality (see del Tufo, et al, 1982). Here, as in other local and national campaigns, black academics and activists, who themselves have written influentially on the nature of institutional racism, and who are the 'organic intellectuals' of this movement, have been heavily involved as collaborators and consultants.

(b) 'policy entrepreneurs': bureaucratic and political:
Realistically, criticisms by parents, particularly black and working class parents, about the educational opportunities offered to their children, are likely to stimulate policy changes only in circumstances where it is in the interests of local councillors and/or professional officers to effect changes. In this context, Ken Young and Naomi Connelly have argued that policies in various LEAs have become racialised in the last few years mainly because of the efforts of 'policy entrepreneurs'. That is, 'officers and councillors who were committed to change and who could make skilful use of such pressures from the community or from central agencies as were to hand' (1981, p.6). Although this is, on the face of it, an attractive interpretation of the dynamics and origins of newly formulated goals of policy in local government, it seems to us heavily flawed. In Troyna's words:

> ..it is difficult to dispute the claim that this appraisal constitutes little more than a truism. To say that policies are formulated at local level because certain individuals recommend their adoption, is to state the obvious. What Young and Connelly have failed to do in their report is to reconstruct the course of events, both locally and nationally, which led to those individuals' "commitment to change". (1984c, p.205).

A wider political context for this trend towards racialisation is, however, provided by writers such as Hatcher and Shallice (1983) and Sivanandan (1983) who have linked it with certain sections on the left of the Labour party. According to this account, these councillors see as part of their constituency a range of 'disadvantaged' groups to whom they can offer access to resources in return for votes. So for Sivanandan the implications for black activists are clear: 'The left wing has been left with the ethnic baby; it does not know in which direction to turn and it is up to us to point them in the right direction' (1983, p.8). But it would seem that some local Labour parties are easier to direct than others. They tend to be controlling areas which contain relatively large black communities with voting strength in certain wards. Most are in areas where one political party does not enjoy traditionally a clear majority at elections - there is either a fairly regular change in political control (e.g. Birmingham) or a 'hung' council such as in Berkshire and Leicestershire. What is also important is that although the racialisation of policy has been initiated generally by Labour party members it tends to emerge

65

publicly as a bi-partisan stance which is accepted and continued if and when Conservatives assume control (we shall return to this point in chapter 5 and spell out its implications more fully). It is important however not to oversimplify and overgeneralise these trends. Local specificity is important. In Liverpool, for example, a particular variety of 'left' politics means the controlling Labour Group defines antiracism in a way which stems from a specific form of class analysis of society. In Sheffield, where the Labour party has customarily been in control, antiracist policies are a new phenomenon and only recently have they figured as part of the political agenda. There are different ways of recognising, developing and legitimising specifically Black political concerns. In Manchester and Greater London for example, there are attempts to foster and strengthen Black participation in mainstream rather than separate local politics. In general however, we can see that the racialisation of policies in local government settings has been influenced greatly by a need to attract black electoral support and to incorporate the communities into routine political activities. With the continuing concentration of black citizens amongst the ranks of the poor, unemployed and the poorly housed electorate their support becomes increasingly more important to those local and national politicians who wish to fight the effects of the restructuring of capital through monetarist policies. The geographical and residential concentration of those who are suffering most under Thatcherism seems to us to provide at least a partial explanation of the local emergence of racialised education policies which contrast sharply with the multicultural concerns that continue to prevail in the overwhelming majority of LEAs.

(c) professional and bureaucratic groups:

Without wishing to be excessively cynical it is clear that bureaucratic groups (such as LEA officers and administrators) may also interpret an emphasis on antiracism in their public policies as being to their advantage. This may well be the case when it comes to the allocation of Section 11 funds to specific LEAs and the deployment of these funds by the Authority's officers.[2] Traditionally these monies have been assigned for ESL provision; however, because of pressure from black groups for curriculum change and mother tongue provision, Section 11 finance can also be used for these initiatives. Clearly, Section 11 money is an extremely valuable means of financing a selective expansion of the local education provisions at a time of general retrenchment and cutbacks. Of course, it need not be used in ways which are labelled antiracist, and most of it is not. Nevertheless, it is easier to provide such new emphases if the cost to the ratepayer is minimal. Like their locally elected counterparts, professional educational officers are vulnerable to complaints from parents that the education system is failing a sizeable number of students. Such criticisms are likely to evoke a more positive reaction if schools and teacher competence, rather than service provision per se, constitutes the focus of concern. In this scenario, in which teachers are said either to hold 'unadmitted' racist attitudes and expectations or retain Anglocentric and outmoded syllabuses, administrators can use Section 11 monies to provide in-service training and curriculum support services. This tactical approach corresponds with Wellman's (1977) claim that whites are adept at understanding racism in ways which do not implicate themselves either in its causes or remedies.

It is important to acknowledge, however, that some teachers - and their professional organisations - have played prominent roles in the advocacy of antiracist education policies. The National Union of Teachers (NUT), for instance, no longer espouses support for multicultural education but advocates, instead, a more forceful approach to the eradication of racism, as its 1981 pamphlet, Combatting Racialism in Schools and its evidence to the Swann Committee the following year, testify. Similarly, the All London Teachers Against Racism and Fascism (ALTARF) and National Association for Multiracial Education (NAME) have developed as campaigning groups. ALTARF was established by a group of radical teachers in 1978 in response to a resurgence of National Front activity. By 1984 the group had organised a number of workshops, produced pamphlets and a book and, with the aid of a grant from the GLC, appointed a full-time worker. NAME, on the other hand, has a much longer history. It grew out of a federation of branches collectively called ATEPO: the Association of Teachers of English to Pupils from Overseas. The first branch had been formed as long ago as 1962 and had been based in the West Midlands. During the early 1970s, however, ATEPO members eschewed their exclusive concern with language matters and recognised the need to situate this issue in a broader framework which would include various race-related themes. Hence, the organisation came to be called NAME and its focus: multiracial/cultural education. By the early 1980s the executive membership and editorial board of NAME's journal realised the inadequacies and spurious bases of the multicultural education approach and initiated a more radical, antiracist line of argument.(3) But the strategic concerns of ALTARF and NAME do not coincide entirely. As the organisations' position statements show, NAME tends to concentrate largely, if not entirely, on racism in education milieux whereas for ALTARF: 'Anti-racist teaching which stops at the classroom door cannot truly be described as anti-racist. We must challenge inside and outside the school, the racism, sexism and class structures which divide us' (1984, p.2). This is subtly different from NAME's objectives as spelt out in its journal: '...the principal aim of the National Association for Multiracial Education is to play an active role in making the changes required in the education system which will further the development of a just society' (Editorial, Multiracial Education. Vol. 12, No. 2, 1984, p.1).

Putting to one side these differences in emphasis, one of the most important results of grassroots teacher pressure emanating from ALTARF, NAME and elsewhere, has been the formulation of school-based antiracist policies which have not only frequently preceded those formulated by LEAs, but have also precipitated action from the Authority. All in all then, these groups seem to have been influential both as mediators between academics and LEAs and as independent pressure groups in their own right.

Acting either as representatives of groups such as ALTARF and NAME or as independent activists, black professionals have also campaigned for the recognition of antiracist perspectives in education. During the 1970s in particular, the 'moral panic' about youth and attendant problems led to a growth in the number of black youth workers whose very appointment underlined the importance of racial matters. According to Gus John (1981) the politicisation of black professionals and their clients led to the emergence of pressure groups which pinpointed local authority connivance and compliance with racism. Alongside these groups were white and black radical teachers who had helped previously to introduce multicultural education perspectives into their schools and who were now 'rewarded' with promotion to specialist inspectorate and advisory positions.(4) As a result they found themselves in a position to challenge the prevailing modes of understanding and interpretation and press for the allocation of money for projects and initiatives beyond the standard multicultural framework.

During the 1970s and '80s it has been possible for professional groups within (and beyond) the education system to demonstrate the failure of existing services to win the support and confidence of a large number of black parents and students. As we showed earlier, the growth of supplementary schooling constitutes the most dramatic illustration of this fact. But calls for action, however rational or justified, do not gain credence automatically; rather, they tend to be successful in contexts which allow other professionals and politicians to accept that the new interpretations make sense and, importantly, are in their own interests. The recent inclusion of racism and institutional racism on the political agenda of a number of LEAs therefore has to be considered in relation to wider social and political changes, the way in which these have been interpreted by professional groups and the extent to which these concepts resonate with professionals' interpretations of the causes and solutions to these changes. And in this broader context the 1981 urban disturbances have to be considered as a contributory cause of racialisation.

(d) Black youth and the 'riots' of '81:
It is difficult to pinpoint precisely the effect of the 1981 disturbances (and their symbolic evocation) as a justification for changing policies. However, amidst the various interpretations for the causes of these disturbances, there was general agreement that the education system could, and should, assume a vital role in preventing their recurrence (see Troyna, 1984a). In his report on the disturbances, for example, Lord Scarman highlighted the responsibility of schools to provide 'suitable educational ... opportunities' for black students. They were also called upon to produce more skilled young workers, and to contribute to harmonious race relations (1981). Since 1981 an increasing number of LEAs has responded to Scarman's call for action by producing explicit policies affirming a commitment to multicultural and (less frequently) antiracist goals. Some LEAs, such as Kirklees, openly admitted the

causal effect of the 'riots' on its approaches and policies. So in the preface to its inter-directorate report on the provision of services for a multi-ethnic community we find the chairman of the working party claiming that:

> Just over a year ago when the Directorate of Educational Services undertook to co-ordinate the Authority's response to the Commission for Racial Equality's document "The Fire Next Time" the Bristol St Paul's incident was the only major instance of protest by the ethnic minority communities that the country had experienced. The Working party has concluded its discussions under the shadow of sporadic outbursts of violence in Brixton, Toxteth and elsewhere, even on a relatively minor scale in Huddersfield. Whatever the reason for these protests, and there is some evidence that they were not triggered off solely by racial discord, it would be prudent to take positive steps to eliminate potential sources of discontent (n.d., p.1).

1981 was also the year in which the parliamentary Select Committee on Race Relations and Immigration implored schools to examine their formal and hidden curriculum to ensure that they provided the means to combat racism and promote equality of opportunity. It warned that '... a failure to act, now the facts are generally known, will cause widespread disappointment and ultimately unrest among the ethnic minority groups of our society' (1981, p.106). The growth of youth unemployment, particularly amongst black youth, the acceptance of Rastafarianism by large numbers of students, and the creation of a moral panic round the issue of mugging have all led to black youth being seen as a 'social time bomb', ready to rebel and cause trouble. The particular ways in which these events are interpreted by state agencies are more likely to lead to control measures such as law and order campaigns, extra policing and particular sorts of Youth Training Schemes. However, they can also provide a setting within which radical policies may find space and acceptance. But despite these prescriptions for action there are profound ambiguities and contradictions in the way the state has responded to race-related matters both before and after the disturbances. At a time of a growing acknowledgement of the pervasiveness of racism (as opposed to individual discriminatory acts) and the acceptance of 'black underachievement' as a policy concern (Rampton, 1981), discriminatory immigration legislation has permitted the harassment of black citizens to continue, almost with impunity (Gordon, 1985). In a context of simultaneous concern and repression, law and order and integration rhetoric, state production of 'aliens' and 'citizens', and so on, the education system has been delegated responsibility for what Murray Edelman (1977) terms 'insoluable problems'. In a very real sense this corresponds with Halsey's characterisation of the education system as 'the waste paper basket of social policy', which we referred to in the previous chapter.

ANTIRACIST EDUCATION : DES, LEAs AND TEACHERS

What is particularly striking about the issue of antiracist education, however, is central government's willingness for LEAs to assume responsibility for its promotion and advancement. That is to say, the DES and Secretary of State have confined their intervention on matters about 'race' and education to rhetoric and statements of principle; they have offered no practical guidance for teachers. Sir Keith Joseph, for example, has made speeches attacking racial bullying and name calling in schools and in March 1984 approved the setting up of a Local Authority Race Relations Exchange to facilitate the spread of information concerning good practice in schools (Daily Telegraph, 22 March 1984). The Race Relations Act 1976 also provides some justification for innovation by LEAs and Sections 17-20 are concerned with discrimination in education. But their purpose is to make certain actions unlawful rather than to prescribe alternatives. Even Section 71 which places a duty on Authorities to 'limit unlawful discrimination and to promote equality of opportunity and good race relations' is a persuasive rather than obligatory clause. It has been used largely to justify existing policies, rather than inspire new ones. As far as central government is concerned therefore, the scenario is one of non-policy making: in spite of the Swann report there remains a refusal to place antiracist education on a national policy agenda. How do we account for this?

In an effort to justify its non-interventionist stance on this issue, the DES has appealed consistently to the decentralised nature of the education system (see chapter 2). This appeal is exceptional because, as we will see later, it takes place at a time when the state is demanding greater control over the local financing of education, examinations, vocational education and what takes place generally in individual schools (DES, 1985). But it is also justified (implicitly, at least) in the following terms. The urban disturbances were confined to a few cities: black radicals operate within certain local areas; black youth unemployment is geographically concentrated; ergo: antiracism is an issue of the inner cities and must be developed by those LEAs affected directly by these phenomena. The devastation of the inner cities, and the consequent manifestation of these problems are associated closely with the present crisis of capitalism and the state's response to this. But the rhetoric of social problems keeps this scenario off the political agenda. A decentralised education system means that local policies are generated in the context of local problems: teachers and schools may be reformed, antiracism may be generated in particular local state arenas, but the national state can continue to assume a pose of 'benign neglect' and distance - delegating responsibility and concern.

Our argument here can be simply stated. The contexts in which antiracist policies are developed at the local level are determined largely by national state policies. The rise in unemployment, cutbacks in local services, emphases on training and 'national needs' and so on, are the most obvious and recent examples. Quite clearly, certain locations are suffering more from the restructuring of capital investment and the international division of labour than others (for discussion, see Child and Paddon, 1984; Merseyside Socialist Research Group, 1980). And it is in these areas that youths, particularly black youths, are especially vulnerable to prolonged unemployment. The state determines the social, economic and ideological contexts within which the schools have to respond to these changes. The decline in the birth rate provides a legitimation for resource cuts, particularly in the inner city, and the worsening of pupil/teacher ratios. The 'needs of industry' becomes the ideological framework within which control over the curriculum is asserted. In an increasingly competitive system for jobs, parental support can be gained for a re-emphasis upon a particular version of 'standards' and vocationalism. Local politicians and administrators either have to develop antiracist policies consonant with these other developments, which means a very particular form of antiracism. Or they can provide a rationale and policies which oppose more than racism - which are part of a resistance to the social effects of the restructuring of capital and the aggressive state of Thatcherism.

Finally, it is also important to recognise the historically developed forms in which education is provided: the taken-for-granted institutional and ideological formations in which antiracist initiatives have to be introduced. Examples of these would include a commitment to a meritocratic system of education in which the majority of students are bound to fail. Another would be the historical development of teacher professionalism and the current attempts by teachers to reassert their autonomy from national and local directives in different policy contexts.

Teacher autonomy, defined in terms of academic freedom in the classroom, is an important basis of status and power and can be used to justify the rejection of outside pressures for change. Troyna and Ball (1985a) have recently described the growing resistance of headteachers, in particular, to LEA prescriptive advice on race-related matters in education. To a greater or lesser extent, this derived from these heads' belief that such advice constitutes a further challenge and threat to their perceived autonomy. Ken Jones (1983) has argued in a similar vein and suggested that the left cannot introduce radical ideas and expect them to spread at a time when teacher autonomy is under threat from the political right. But the issue of autonomy is only one of the problems associated with teachers' receptivity to the principles and ideals of antiracism. Another is their perception of antiracism as an overtly political matter which is divisive, causes resentment among students and parents and, therefore, has no place in traditionally 'non-political' curricula. This is an argument put forcibly by Michael Banton (1983); and the empirical work carried out by Troyna and Ball (1985b) with headteachers and their staff confirms the prevalence of this view.

But outright hostility and opposition from teachers is probably less important than inertia and indifference. Troyna (1985a) has shown how few teachers prioritise antiracist education as a matter of concern; a point also touched on by Hatcher and Shallice:

Within the school the demands of examination syllabuses, the hostility of heads and inspectors, governors and other teachers, the simple pressures of time and the unsympathetic response of pupils themselves can all militate powerfully against progressive innovation (1983, p.14).

Given this scenario and inbuilt systems of professional inertia, why should any groups of teachers or administrators adopt antiracist initiatives? Clearly political and moral commitment to racial justice is a motivating factor for some. For others, their own teaching experience and the circumstances of their professional lives will be sufficient to show that established approaches (including those derived from a multicultural perspective) have done little to undermine racial inequality and hostility in the classroom. As Jones and Kimberley (1982) note, teachers have difficulty in coming to terms with the implicit or explicit hostility of students. Paul Willis (1977) has suggested that teachers need 'explanations in use' of their day-to-day problems. As their authority is moral rather than coercive they need the consent of their students to the processes of schooling. With most students they exchange guidance for control and knowledge for respect. With others, this guidance and knowledge is rejected; the bargain is broken and, perhaps, in need of 'antiracist repair'. This is not meant to be a flippant or cynical observation. Troyna and Ball (1985b) have demonstrated clearly in this specific context that if teachers do not feel they have a problem (i.e. no black students, in their terms) then there is minimal incentive to reappraise and reconstitute their curriculum or pedagogy.

So it is teachers in inner-city, ethnically mixed schools who are attempting to cope with tensions generated by forces beyond their control, for whom antiracist education policies make most immediate (and pragmatic) sense. It is this group which throws up the pioneers, initiators and supporters of change.

How, then, can we cohere into a unified framework the various and complex factors which have stimulated this form of racialisation. LEAs can be seen as sites of struggle where attempts to reconcile political pressures, parental demands, teacher and student activities, and administrative and institutional inertia are acted out. But these struggles take shape and form in response to material and ideological contexts which, themselves, are determined by national and international developments over which they have no control. The precise forms in which these local struggles produce antiracist initiatives therefore need to be determined empirically for as Fenton (1982) informs us, the meaning of antiracism is stipulated in practice not in theories. This is our concern in the following two chapters: what types of antiracist education policies have developed in particular local areas.

FOOTNOTES

1. A similar point has been made in the Swann report. Committee members have attributed considerable significance to their 1981 interim report in facilitating 'a quite marked shift in opinion, both within the education system and society at large, on the propriety of openly discussing this issue (i.e. racism)' (1985, p.10).

2. Section 11 of the Local Government Act (1966) enabled the Home Office to reimburse LEAs at the rate of 50 per cent (later 75 per cent) of expenditure for 'special provision in the exercise of any of their functions in consequence of the presence of substantial numbers of immigrants from the Commonwealth whose languages and culture differ'.   The conditions regulating Section 11 grants were revised in 1982 although they are still geared specifically to provision for the benefit of persons of New Commonwealth origin.

3. This was confirmed officially at the organisation's 1985 annual conference where the membership voted overwhelmingly for a change in name.   The acronym, NAME, now stands for the National Anti-racist Movement in Education.

4. Such an example can be found in the ILEA. As we pointed out in chapter 2, the Senior Inspector for Multiethnic Education previously taught in Tulse Hill school where he had initiated a Black Studies course. Similar examples can be found at inspectorate and advisory level in various LEAs, up and down the country.

Chapter Five

LOCAL EDUCATION AUTHORITY ANTIRACIST POLICIES

We now want to put some flesh on the bones of our analysis by specifying in detail local examples of benign racialisation in educational policy. How many LEA policy documents can be designated legitimately as antiracist is a matter of conjecture, however. It hinges not only on when policies are considered but also on how antiracism is defined. For instance, Gerry German writing in 1983 claimed that 21 Authorities had published documents declaring a commitment to antiracism. But Mullard and his colleagues disagree. In 1982 they wrote to all LEAs and found from the 110 replies received that only about ten percent had some explicit antiracist aims (Mullard, et al, 1983). Despite these variations one point is clear: only a small minority of Authorities has acknowledged this shift in their thinking and appraisal of their educational services. But is is a growing minority and since Mullard completed his survey the local trend towards racialisation has accelerated. Indeed, our analysis will concentrate largely on policy documents produced after Mullard's survey; that is, post-1982.

Unlike multicultural education - which attracted academic critiques like honey attracts bees - there has been little theoretical analysis of the racialisation of educational debates. Therefore there are few existing guidelines or theoretical frameworks waiting to be explored. For that reason we decided to focus attention on the documents and policies produced by seven LEAs:(1) Berkshire; Bradford: Brent; Haringey: ILEA; Manchester and Sheffield. These LEAs are acknowledged both within and outside their boundaries as having explicit antiracist commitments, although they are at different stages of the formulation of their final policies. It is important to note, for example, that at the time of writing (early 1985) Manchester and Sheffield had only recently initiated this process and their policies were still in embryonic form.

Our analysis constitutes 'grounded research' ; the aim is to illustrate through comparative study the distinctive features of policies generated in specific local contexts, and their common concerns which reflect broader, national developments. As in earlier chapters the focus is on the conceptual and ideological frameworks in which these policies are situated. Now it is clear that the ideological shift from multiculturalism to antiracism requires some form of political legitimation in the local context and we shall begin by looking at the processes through which this legitimation has been achieved in the seven LEAs. Following on from this we shall look at the different ways in which policy-makers in these Authorities have theorised the complex, even diffuse, models of racism, antiracism and institutional racism and consider the policy proposals which have stemmed from them. Amongst other things this will enable us to tease out continuities and discontinuities between antiracist and multicultural models of education change. Finally, in order to facilitate a comparative understanding of how these LEAs have conceptualised and operationalised notions of antiracist education we shall propose a series of models based on: (i) the style of policy intervention; (ii) understandings of racism implicit in policies; (iii) the content and emphases of policies: and (iv) the major themes implicit in policy discourse.

THE LEGITIMATION PROCESS:

What is immediately striking about these policies is that they are presented, explicitly or otherwise, as a cross-party commitment. That is to say, despite the fact that the majority are produced in Labour-controlled Authorities (as we noted in chapter 4) the policies are not associated directly with the controlling party. What is more, a reading of the documents suggests that there have been no major disputes about their adoption. This apparent political consensus is important in our understanding of the way these policies are presented. It helps to explain, for instance, why general political rights and representation are emphasised in preference to the inadequacies of particular political philosophies or practices either at local or national government level. The 1978 Haringey policy provides an illustrative example of this: 'Every individual has a right to expect and to receive the benefits of full civil liberties, personal respect, freedom and equality of opportunity in employment, housing and education.' ILEA (4) makes an even stronger case for unity of interests by insisting that an antiracist policy is for the public good because there is a tradition of 'tolerance' and 'opposition to injustice' in British society, which will support initiatives to dismantle racial inequalities and disadvantages in education.

On the face of it, Sheffield might have been expected to be the exception to this general pattern. There, the Labour party has a long history of local political control. Furthermore, the current Labour Council - far more radical than its predecessors - has opposed consistently and publicly the Conservative government's monetarist policies. Even in Sheffield, however, the LEA's antiracist policy displays no sign of party allegiance.(2) These apparent contradictions in the local Labour parties' policy and approach can also be found in Manchester where a left-wing Labour council was elected in May 1984. With ILEA and Sheffield it has spelt out its opposition to the national government on a number of occasions. Nevertheless, its manifesto commitment to establish Manchester as 'a City at the centre of opposition to racism' (Manchester (7), p.9) has not been operationalised in party political terms.

This general determination to ensure that policies are not linked with a particular political party has meant that in the published policy inter-party disputes about the content, nature or thrust of the document are, at most, infrequent and fragmented. Perhaps even more importantly in the context of our argument is that there are discernible parallels in the way multicultural and antiracist education policies have been legitimated. The apparent absence of major inter-party disagreement and the commitment to cross-party support for LEA antiracist education policies reflect precisely the trends we uncovered in the formulation of ILEA's 1977 multiethnic education policy.

We can interpret this largely in terms of the attempt by all major parties to attract the black vote via the representation of their interests and a public approval of uniform citizenship rights. This is a tricky road to tread because of the nagging threat of alienating white voters in the process. For this reason the rights of all citizens are stressed in the policies - an approach and doctrine which, from a pragmatic view at least, all parties need to be seen to endorse.

The clearest example of this can be found in Bradford where the inclusion of racism on the education policy agenda has been initiated by some Conservative councillors. The impetus for change has not been difficult to detect. As one Conservative councillor admitted:

> Any political party that tells you that it's doing things for purely altruistic reasons is either a fool or a liar. Clearly both political parties or three political parties are looking to take a chunk of the black and Asian vote. Speaking as a Conservative, I am realistic in realising that at the moment my party is not receiving a great number of Asian votes (quoted in Morris, et al, 1984, p.8).

The removal of antiracist initiatives from the party political arena is important also in the struggle for educational legitimation of policies. Most teachers continue to view education as 'non-political' and equate political ideologies in education as forms of indoctrination. The absence of political partisanship in the policies might therefore facilitate their acceptance by teachers, at least in principle.

Cross-party support for antiracist policies is only one of the strands of the legitimation process. Another relates to the acceptance of policies by those who are 'racially' oppressed. Thus there is a need to establish consultative procedures with local black communities either during the policy's evolution or as a means of securing support for the final version of the document. Again, however, the nature and extent of consultation are rarely specified in the public documents. From what we are led to believe consultation, per se, constitutes community legitimation for these policies. This may or may not be true. Without knowing who has been consulted, at what stage and to what effect, the role of consultative procedures in the formulation of policies remains a mystery. After all, consultation is a nebulous term which may be operationalised as part of the policy-making processes in various ways. The implication, of course, is that consultation is synonymous with referendum procedures; but it is not. As Kenneth Brooksbank makes clear, consultation,

> ..... is not a process by which views are collected and the persons consulting are committed to the majority view... In educational administration, consultation is the process by which those authorised to make a decision convey the nature of their proposals or the facts underlying those proposals to those affected by them. They do so while ready to change what they are doing, in response to what is said during the consultative process; but they are not committed to such changes (1980, pp. 221-222).

On the face of it, ILEA policy-makers seem to have been most sensitive and responsive to the importance of consultation. In ILEA (2) there is criticism of previous initiatives and provision within and beyond the Authority precisely because they were developed by white professionals with minimal contributions from black parents or voluntary groups. In contrast, it is claimed that the new policies have been developed in collaboration with black groups, campaigning organisations such as ALTARF and NAME and with teachers in schools where antiracist policies already exist.

It is, however, the views of black social scientists such as Chris Mullard, Maureen Stone, Gajendra Verma and Sivanandan which are represented most fully in the policy package. Thus the relevant section in ILEA (2) concludes: 'The black perspective on the role of the education system has identified three priorities: (i) anti-racist teaching; (ii) proper representation of black interests and (iii) an ending of black underachievement' (p.16 Emphasis added). Remarkably, there is no mention of parental groups, the ILEA/CRC consultative committee or the likelihood that a mixture of views exist within the black communities of Inner London.

Despite these criticisms, the ILEA documents provide far more detail on consultative issues than other LEAs. For instance, the Brent documents offer no details about the origins of the policy other than suggesting that the appointment of a black adviser for multicultural education in 1980 constituted the catalyst for change. In Berkshire, only the blandest statements are produced; yet they conceal several years of intense conflict and dispute. We are told through its General Policy paper that an advisory committee had been set up which produced a discussion document subsequently endorsed by the Education Committee. We are also informed of consultations between LEA representatives and Afro-Caribbean and Asian organisations, teachers, heads and lecturers: but again, we know nothing about the nature of these consultations, how they were established and, most importantly, how far the resulting documents reflected and incorporated the views expressed during these consultative procedures. We have to go elsewhere for any light to be shed on these matters (del Tufo, et al, 1982).

In the absence of 'inside' information it is possible only to speculate on forms of consultation and the claims to legitimacy embodied in the wording of policy documents. Bradford's documents (2/82 and 6/83) provide no details of the lengthy and conflictual background to their publication. However, as a third of local school students are of South Asian origin and are predominantly Muslim, it is reasonable to assume that the incipient and existing cultural conflicts between parents and teachers provide the context for the policy development. What is interesting about both Bradford documents is that they present headteachers with a series of instructions which they are expected to accept. These instructions represent the outcome of negotiations between the LEA and (mainly) Muslim groups, and include policies concerning the rights of parents to withdraw their children from assemblies and RE lessons; regulations governing school clothing and dietary provision; and invitations for local religious leaders to enter the schools. The policies are presented in a framework of legitimate parental demands – the outcome of the first 'form of official contact between various ethnic minority organisations and the Council,' according to Michael Whittaker, Bradford's Senior Policy Adviser (quoted in Morris, et al, 1984, p.9). In fact, the policy package contains the selective legitimation of some of the local communities' demands. Nor does this differential incorporation and legitimation of community views bear any obvious relationship to the level of support for certain issues. After all the LEA took a considerable time in responding to the anxieties of the Parents Action Committee of Drummond Middle School where the headteacher, Raymond Honeyford, has made public his opposition to antiracist education and articulated a patronising attitude towards black people (see chapter 6). Despite the fact that the school comprises 86 percent black students, that a 600 signature petition demanding the removal of Honeyford has been handed to the Director of Education and there was a school strike in June 1984 in which 70 percent of the students stayed away, the LEA's response has been hesitant and ambiguous (Foster-Carter, 1985). The Authority has also refused consistently to accede to the Muslim Parents Association's demand for independent, single-sex schools despite the MPA's appeals to relevant sections of the 1944 and 1980 Education Acts. The Authority maintains that demands for the retention of Muslim culture must be negotiated for and satisfied within existing LEA services and school structures. What complicates an already complex picture are the demands made by the Asian Youth Movement in Bradford. Some of these demands correspond with those of other parental and religious groups, some are in contradistinction to them. It is from within this heterogeneity of views that the LEA selects what shall be included in its policy. In the process it legitimates particular community interests and perspectives and dismisses others.

So far we have looked at those Authorities where, to a greater or lesser degree, the local black communities have had some say in the formulation of policies. In Manchester and Sheffield, however, the initiatives in policy formulation have been taken largely by politicians and professional officers who have consulted the communities mainly for an endorsement of, not substantive contributions to their policies. This has been the established pattern in Manchester since 1978 and has continued with its more recent draft policy on antiracism. This document was circulated to 95 local community groups for support; few bothered to reply, however. Perhaps partly in response to this the Authority has reconsidered its general strategy of consultation. In Sheffield the initial discussion document was produced mainly by professionals in the Authority's multicultural support group and subsequent consultations with teachers and school governors about implementation strategies led to the formulation of a draft document in May 1984.

All of this leads us to conclude that the rhetoric of policy documents conceals inter- and intra-party political differences and conflicts arising from, on the one hand, the ideological and practical concerns of (mainly white) professionals and politicians and, on the other, those concerns expressed by black community representatives. The result: policy presentations which allow for the unacknowledged, selective legitimation of particular forms of pressure and a general agreement that policies are for the 'public good'.

OLD WINE IN NEW BOTTLES?

One of our main contentions in this book is that, as they are currently constituted, antiracist education policies do not represent such a radical break with the past as policy-makers would have us believe. Of course, there are some departures from earlier formulations, appraisal and provision: but as we can now show, there are also significant continuities. A specification of the theoretical and policy paradigms of these documents will allow us to consider the particular forms in which the racialisation of policy and debate is proceeding, as well as helping us to tease out continuities and discontinuities in theories and practice.

(a) Policy rhetoric and goals:

In different ways, Berkshire, Brent, ILEA and Manchester suggest that earlier policy formulations based on assimilationist, integrationist and pluralist conceptions problematised black students, their cultures and families. In Berkshire's summary leaflet, Education for Equality, we are told that policies which derived from these perspectives were negative, harmful, insensitive, inaccurate, weak, biased, uncritical and racist. Now whether this summary negation of earlier approaches to race-related matters in education is an accurate appraisal of the effects of earlier policies is impossible to establish. But it is used to support a rejection of such policies and a commitment to ensure that such assumptions and developments find no place in the new policies. Collectively it is asserted that the focus must not be on black pathology, special needs (defined by whites), or ethnocentric evaluations of different cultures. Instead, policies and initiatives must crystallize around the themes of white power, racial inequality and discrimination, and black participation in educational decision-making processes. The central ideological shift is from provision based on black needs (defined by whites) to one based on white responsibility for and culpability in racial inequality and injustice. It seems to us, however, that these simplistic portrayals of a radical shift from the past are misleading. Continuities are rather more obvious and given our understanding of education change, more likely.

As we have indicated, justifications for the new policies imply a critique of the existing situation. It should follow logically therefore that <u>what</u> in education is in need of change must be made explicit. But in most cases there are no clear statements specifying the nature of <u>educational</u> inequalities. In the third document of the ILEA policy package there is a reference to wider inequalities such as the comparatively poorer jobs, housing, health and general life chances of Blacks. But the emphasis on equality and justice <u>implies</u> rather than demonstrates the educational inequalities to be tackled. In ILEA (1) there is detailed reference to differential achievement levels along ethnic, class and gender lines but these data are not adduced for support in documents (4) and (5) where race-related policies are discussed directly. In all the relevant LEA documents we analysed, racism is specified as the evil to be remedied; it is the catch-all phrase for most of what is wrong with education, and responsibility for its continued existence is said to be located at school, local authority and wider societal levels. In consequence, justifications for the policy initiative assume one or more of the following forms: (a) the inadequacies and misconceptions of previous policy statements; (b) the need for schools to respond positively and clearly to the development of a multiracial society; and (c) the commitment to ensure that such a society will become fairer, more equal and just.

Berkshire's policy documents provide a clear example of the third justificatory approach. Here the aim is to promote racial equality and justice by opposing and dismantling racism. The rationale takes three forms. First, racism is morally wrong. Second, it is against the longterm interests of all because it leads to social unrest. Third, it gives people a false and distorted view of their own identity and history.

The Brent documents proceed roughly along the same lines. In the first of its two booklets the goal is spelt out in the following way: 'The ultimate aim of the intended educational innovation in Brent is the fundamental improvement in the life chances of children in our schools' (p.4). The Authority acknowledges the existence of racial inequality and disadvantages, proposes that schools have supported and perpetuated such iniquities and insists that this pattern must be broken. But again, the <u>direct</u> relationship between schools and inequalities is assumed. Although Haringey's 1978 document is shorter and more sharply focussed than the others in our sample, it is also geared towards the related aims of the development of a harmonious multiracial society, the development of self-respect and respect for others, and 'the truth'.

The remaining LEAs (i.e. Bradford, Sheffield and Manchester) state their policy goals more succinctly. Either these are taken to be self-evident or their justifications can be found in supporting documentation. In Sheffield (3), for instance, the following aims are outlined:

(i)   To promote understanding, throughout the education service, of the different cultures found in Britain today, and to prepare all individuals for life in a "plural" society where diversity is welcomed.

(ii)   To define and combat discrimination and racism, whether overt, unintentional or institutional.

(iii)   To meet the needs of all children with particular regard to their cultural background, religion and language. This may require positive discrimination.

These derive from Sheffield's 1982 discussion document where an antiracist ideology is contrasted sharply with ethnocentric orientations.

Since 1981, Manchester LEA has been developing an antiracist policy which comprises two significant strands. The first, which began in 1981-2, requested local educational institutions to formulate an Institutional Policy on Racism. This was expected to include reports of racist incidents and evidence of the development of antiracist curriculum strategies which would enable, amongst other things, 'each individual to enjoy, cherish and appreciate living in a culturally plural society.' More recently this initiative has been supplemented by an antiracist statement which embraces aims taken to be self-evidently reasonable:

Manchester Education Committee employ over 15,000 people within this city. As an employer committed to confronting racism and its damaging effects on all Mancunians the Committee expect their employees to uphold this commitment. All employees, both non-teaching and teaching and of every grade, are expected to contribute fully to an education service founded on equal rights, equal opportunities and mutual respect.

The Committee expect their employees to behave in a non-racist way towards the public, other employees, students and pupils. More than this, employees are encouraged to be critical of and to help change institutional practices and procedures that work against equality.

Racist abuse, harassment and discrimination is not acceptable. Employees must know that such behaviour will be subject to disciplinary action possibly leading to dismissal. (1984).

Finally, we come to Bradford's policy, the aims of which can be summarised as follows:

(i)   To seek ways of preparing all children and young people for life in a multicultural society.

(ii)   To counter racism and racist attitudes, and the inequalities and discrimination which results from them.

(iii)   To build on and develop the strengths of cultural and linguistic diversity.

(iv)   To respond sensitively to the special needs of minority groups. (1982).

Bradford's memorandum 6/83 states, on the one hand, that schools have a special responsibility for enhancing racial understanding, tolerance and individual respect. On the other, that they have a responsibility to ensure that children within their care understand that racialist behaviour and attitudes which endanger these objectives will not be tolerated. Schools are also presented with detailed instructions on how these goals might be achieved. Finally, the LEA specifies a number of other policy objectives which include minimising parent/teacher conflict and preventing the rise of separate schooling. In support of the latter it asserts: 'The authority is greatly concerned to maintain a shared educational experience for all the children in Bradford.'

What common features can we tease out from this overview of LEA policy statements and documents? Following on from our earlier observation it is clear that antiracist policy aims are firmly embraced within a moral and, to a lesser degree, educational framework. Even when political concerns are touched on they are presented in a depoliticised and moral form: justice, harmony, plural democracy, citizenship rights and so on are the key concepts in this context. Such moral justifications necessarily connote particular assumptions about the unitary nature of citizenship particularly, and society in general. Deliberately or otherwise, they play down divisions and subsume separate interests within the 'symbolic political language' (to use Murray Edelman's phrase (1977)) of 'equality of opportunity for all'. This is interesting because we saw in chapter 3 that academic and political analyses of the terms, racism and institutional racism, focused on those very issues which policy statements oversimplify; namely, the economic basis of racism and its ideological function of preserving the privileges of Whites against Blacks. How then do policy-makers reconcile their consensual justifications for antiracist education with their emphasis on institutional racism as the key explanatory concept?

(b) Models of racism, institutional racism and antiracism:

Some Authorities, such as Berkshire and the ILEA, provide a theoretical exposition of the term racism. Others deploy 'racism' in a taken-for-granted manner so that it is left to the reader to distil a meaning from policy recommendations. Let us look at these differential approaches to and uses of the concept in more detail.

According to the first of the Brent booklets, racism is 'endemic in the normal British education system' (p.20). Racism, in this context, denotes an ideological system which, prima facie, assumes white superiority over Blacks either explicitly or more subtly through the omission of alternative cultural standards. Following on from this, white teachers are said to internalise racism from society and transmit it to their students as part of their routine pedagogy. The unintentional and unadmitted nature of this process is typified as institutional racism. Thus: 'Teachers are supporting and defending a system which is inherently racist because it is based on inappropriate assumptions' (Brent (1), p.36). From this standpoint the logical solution is attitude change: the means: racism awareness courses so that teachers no longer collude with racialist practices and unintended cultural racism. What is missing from this formulation is a critical appraisal of the role of individual attitudes in the creation and maintenance of inequalities, a point we developed in earlier chapters.

Turning to the policies of Berkshire and the ILEA we find a much wider and sophisticated understanding of the term. In the first of Berkshire's documents, racism is said to consist of 'the interaction between three separate components: an uneven distribution of power and influence; discriminatory practices, procedures and customs: and the prejudiced beliefs and attitudes of indivdiuals, both conscious and unconscious' (p.4). For the ILEA: 'Racism is a shorthand term for this combination of discriminatory practices, unequal relations and structures of power and negative beliefs and attitudes' (ILEA (3), p.21). What conventionally is termed institutional racism, (namely, the routine procedures of the school) is implicit within the Berkshire and ILEA definitions. What is more, for both LEAs the purpose of defining and analysing racism is clear: to facilitate the development of policies which tackle directly racial inequalities and injustice. Such policies are labelled antiracist. In Berkshire they are geared towards breaking the 'vicious cycles and spirals' which serve to maintain white power. In the ILEA they are designed to eliminate racism in its various manifest forms: structural, political, ideological, cultural and historical. We noted in chapter 3 how the terms, racism and institutional racism, were frequently deployed to embrace an array of power relationships, patterns of behaviour and individual attitudes. There we expressed doubts about the theoretical validity and proposed policy direction of such an approach. We underline those doubts here. Although this framework rightly emphasises the generation of racism outside the school, the way it is presented makes few direct links with achievable educational goals.

The detailed exposition of the term, racism, found in the formal policy documents of Berkshire and the ILEA is the exception rather than the rule. In Manchester, for instance, analysis along these lines only appears in a supporting document, Reviewing the Secondary Curriculum (1982). In the introduction, racism is defined and identified in three distinctive forms. First, 'voluntary individual racism' which refers to the activities of contemporary fascist groups such as the National Front and British Movement. Second, 'involuntary individual racism' which, according to the authors, 'is a condition, like sexism, in which one carries round, unconsciously, certain prejudices towards whole groups of people, to their detriment.' Finally, 'Institutional racism' which is defined as: 'written or unwritten practices or rules in institutions of any kind, which hinder or prevent the progress of black people and which are founded on attitudes of racial superiority'. In the school setting, the celebration of Christmas and the neglect of the major festivals in the Islam and Hindu religions is offered as an example of institutional racism. Once again we are alerted to a wide range of policy reforms necessary to eradicate such assumptions and practices. The LEA's 1984 antiracist statement builds on this analysis and enjoins employees to behave in a non-racist way, specifying racial abuse, harassment and discrimination as forms of unacceptable behaviour.

Neither Bradford nor Haringey spend much time delineating the meaning of racism or specifying in any detail the various forms in which it is manifested. In both LEAs there is a sharp focus on racialist behaviour, defined in Bradford as: 'any hostile or offensive act or expression by a person of one racial group against another racial group, or any incitement to commit such an act, where there is an indication that the motivation is racial dislike or hatred' (Bradford (2)). In this Authority antiracism denotes both an acceptance of community cultural values and opposition to teacher and student racism.

The various models and definitions of racism operationalised by these seven LEAs, though incorporating some distinctive features, nevertheless are amenable to categorisation. Clara Mulhern (1980, pp.3–4) has already attempted this and her specification of the way racism is used in educational discourse and debate is relevant here. For Mulhern, then, educationists tend to use racism in one or more of the following ways:

(i)   A moral emphasis which treats racism as offensive and looks to consciousness raising as an important antiracist activity.

(ii)   An educational emphasis in which racism is discussed largely in terms of ignorance; consequently, re-education of an intellectual kind via antiracist curricula is posited as the most appropriate strategy.

(iii)   A political analysis which emphasises historical and contemporary manifestations of inequality and oppression.

To these categories we would add:

(iv)   A behavioural emphasis which concentrates on the racialist actions of individuals in specific circumstances. Attempts are made to control these in the interests of racial equality and harmony.

To a greater or lesser extent, these emphases are present in each of the documents we have described in this chapter. Furthermore, they are compatible with the different foci of policies; that is, who or what is specified as the target of change: students, teachers, the education system or the broader social and political context.

(c) Priorites for action:

We can now move from an analysis of the theoretical predicates of policies and look at the relationship between specified aims and practices. By this we do not mean the substantive impact of policies on local educational institutions; rather, we are concerned with the intended outcomes of the policies and the steps taken by LEAs to expedite these outcomes. It should be noted that the relationship between LEA policies and intended practices is not as clear-cut as some might assume. For instance, whether or not the policies are intended to be change-agents in schools, first and foremost, is a matter of dispute (see Richardson, 1983; Troyna and Ball, 1985a). It is, therefore, important to clarify these intended and desired aims before an evaluation of their success or efficacy can even be considered.

In his overview of LEA policies on multiracial education, Dorn made the point that there is considerable overlap in the provisions stemming from such initiatives. Thus: 'ESL, mother tongue, curriculum development, Section 11 funds, teacher training (particularly in-service) and ethnic statistics are uniform concerns' (1983, p.4). These matters also figure prominently on the agenda for reforms in our sample of Authorities, indicating again the continuities in policy formulations. It is important to note that all authorities intend to or have recruited specialist teachers funded by Section 11 money. Berkshire for example specifies in its action programme a language support service which includes community languages and a community education team. Sheffield's list of specialists includes an adviser, home/school liaison teachers and a multicultural development centre. Brent, in 1983, established a Curriculum Development Support Unit and six cultural liaison teachers. All these posts have been created on the basis of new Section 11 guidelines published in circular 97/1982 which stated that designated posts should meet the needs of commonwealth immigrants whose language and/or customs differ from the rest of the community (sic). However, Authorities such as Berkshire and the ILEA also pledge to recruit and promote more black teachers and to ensure a greater presence of Blacks on school governing bodies. There is also a growing tendency in LEAs such as Brent and Manchester to encourage schools to nominate a member of staff to liaise between the school and the Authority's support service and stimulate initiatives along antiracist lines in the curriculum.

A major point of departure from Dorn's list is the attempt by a small number of LEAs to establish staff codes of conduct. In Manchester the aim is to achieve this through disciplinary procedures; in Bradford the approach is through administrative directives. Obviously this is a controversial move and has excited a number of teachers and their unions who see it as an encroachment on their professional standing and autonomy (see Troyna and Ball, 1985a).

Most policies are concerned more with proposing changes in local schools than with reformulating the routine practices and activities of County Halls and their various departments. Each educational institution in Inner London for example is instructed to appraise its formal and informal curriculum, develop and publicise an antiracist policy and provide the Authority with detailed accounts of how and when the policy will be implemented. Details on the sorts of questions schools and colleges should consider are outlined in the ILEA's aide-memoire for the Inspectorate. These range from the straightforward - 'What provision is made to communicate with parents whose mother tongue is not English?' - to the vague: 'Do members of staff see pupils as individuals, while at the same time appreciating the importance of their adherence to particular ethnic cultural groups?'

Berkshire has approached the issue of school reappraisal slightly differently in so far as a series of questions is integrated formally into the policy documents. Additionally, specific themes and concepts are recommended for inclusion in school curricula: diversity; similarity; justice; civilisation; migration; racism; colonialism; resistance and interdependence. By far the lengthiest document is provided for Brent teachers. This emphasises the relative freedom accorded to teachers in the UK's decentralised education system and the fundamental part teachers must assume if the LEA's policy is to have an effect in local schools and colleges. At the same time, the policy-makers stress the part teachers play in the legitimation and perpetuation of racism. The booklet provides a range of questions designed to make explicit both routine educational assumptions and the philosophical bases of curriculum and pedagogy. The aim is to facilitate changes in attitudes and the practices which stem from them.

The questions provided for teachers in these LEAs give some flavour of the changes desired and encouraged by policy-makers. In reality, however, it is difficult to crystallize these aims in any meaningful or constructive manner, largely because the lists are so lengthy, their focus so broad and their wording often vague. Perhaps most significantly, the LEAs do not provide any criteria by which the success or otherwise of the prescribed changes might be evaluated.

(d) Mobilising allies:

Our final point draws attention to the relationship between antiracist initiatives in local education departments and parallel developments in other service sections in the Authority. It would seem that the initiatives we have identified tend to occupy a place in a broader Local Authority (LA) antiracist strategy. Most of the LAs we have been discussing have established Equal Opportunity Units and have introduced policies aimed at ending discrimination against women, the handicapped and Gays. In Manchester, for example, each department is expected to develop parallel policies and report back to a centrally-based Equal Opportunities Committee. In Sheffield, an independent Ethnic Minorities Unit has been established in the Chief Executive's department. Its purpose is to initiate a more focussed and co-ordinated attack on racism throughout the City Council. As we pointed out before, its impending antiracist statement will be endorsed by all the major political parties represented in the City Council and will be based on the proposition that: 'racial discrimination is a direct result of racism and is a problem which cannot be simply equated with class, sex, urban deprivation, inner city malaise or with linguistic or cultural differences.'

As our earlier discussion about consultation suggested, some LEAs present the antiracist issue as a means of involving local residents in the process of policy development and implementation. From this perspective, it may be seen as a cautious move along the road towards greater community involvement in education. This is certainly the way Frances Morrell, leader of the ILEA sees it (1984). Because school governors are assigned a vital part in the implementation of policy initiatives the imperative in a number of LEAs is to ensure that governing bodies represent accurately the interests of local residents or, at least, are kept informed of the demands and expectations of those residents. To facilitate this process Manchester LEA aims to establish District Committees to channel community views to the Authority.

In Bradford, a range of prescriptive advisory notes have been issued to schools informing them of the various ways in which community involvement in the schools might be enhanced. These include the translation of school notices and letters into local community languages, the provision of interpreters and the acceptance of Imams into school.

In the ILEA a commitment to community education has been expressed publicly through the acceptance of David Hargreaves' report, Improving Secondary Schools (1984). Some might say that the report has deprioritised antiracist matters. But this may be a premature judgement. As we have seen, most versions of antiracism require the involvement of those suffering from racial oppression in the formulation, implementation and monitoring of policies. Those policies which focus on racism as a disciplinary offence and which call for the itemisation of racist incidents often need the active involvement and co-operation of parents and community organisations to bring these to the attention of the LEA. Similarly, where education policies constitute part of a wider emphasis on equal opportunities, different sections of the local communities may be drawn into the struggles of specific groups. Unfortunately, the details of how LEAs aim to achieve this involvement is not spelt out in the policies.

MODELS OF LEA ANTIRACIST EDUCATION POLICIES:

We have provided the basis for 'grounded research' in this chapter by comparing a number of LEAs in different parts of the country on a range of specific orientations toward the development of antiracist education. At one level, specific local characteristics are important. The variations in, say, local demography, the political strengths and mix of local community groups and the competing ideological and commonsense understandings of race-related issues combine with an economic and bureaucratic history to produce unique patterns in approach and provision. At a more general level, however, it is possible to develop models of antiracism not simply for their own sake but to facilitate generalisations and comparisons as well as preparing the ground for theoretical explorations.

Because we have scrutinised several dimensions of antiracist education policies it would be a gross distortion to attempt to include these in a single, overarching model. Let us begin therefore with the style of policy intervention.

It has been argued elsewhere that the vast majority of LEA multicultural/ethnic/racial policies can be characterised first by their laissez-faire or permissive mode of intervention, and second by their emphasis on vague rather than explicit exhortations for action (Troyna and Ball, 1985a). In other words, LEA officers and members working within this paradigm were willing to devolve responsibility for the development of multicultural/ethnic/racial education in schools to individual headteachers and their staff. At the same time their aims were packaged in grandiose and inexplicit language. A clear example of this can be found in Lothian's 1983 policy which asked teachers to ensure that: 'the ethos within the various educational establishments is conducive to harmonious social relationships among all pupils and students.' Our reading of the seven LEA antiracist policy statements suggests that this permissive mode has been eschewed largely in favour of a more interventionist and demanding approach. The policies developed in Bradford, the ILEA and Manchester for example, all require evidence of the antiracist response of local education institutions. What is more, because some, like the ILEA, have imposed delivery dates (in the ILEA) it is implied that methods of assessing responses will be introduced. However, whilst the style of policy intervention might differentiate multicultural from antiracist stances, the nature of instructions to institutions has remained vague and general. Even in Bradford and Manchester, where the emphasis is on proscribing racialist behaviour, policy-makers have not specified the range of behaviours to be included nor have they indicated how and when disciplinary procedures will be used as sanctions. All in all this suggests that whilst antiracist policies are more prescriptive and proscriptive than their multicultural forerunners most still remain inexplicit.

A second model hinges on the main concerns of the policies; how do policy-makers interpret the origins of racism in education in a way which informs the foci of their policies and documents? Diagram 1 gives some clues to their main emphases.

Diagram 1:

Understandings of Racism in LEA Policies

Nature of racism		LEA
Political/economic:	Racism in education as a consequence of the structural features of society	Berkshire; ILEA
Ideological:	(i) Individual attitudes/ commonsense racism	Haringey
	(ii) Knowledge institution-alised in the curriculum	Brent
Cultural:	Cultural differences defined as illegitimate or ignored	Bradford
Behavioural:	(i) Right wing groups or particular pupils	Bradford
	(ii) Of teachers and other LEA employees	Manchester.

Of course, some LEAs have developed strategies for coping with all these dimensions. Some may also have acknowledged the theoretical veracity of one particular interpretation of racism but have discarded it for another for politically expedient reasons. The point we want to make is that these examples illustrate the principal emphases of the major policy documents. The third model concerns the substantive content of policies and the issues around which they cohere. Diagram 2 illustrates the differing policy options.

Diagram 2:

Antiracist Policy Options

Focus		Content
	i	Racist incidents – namecalling graffiti attacks
White Racism	ii	Attitude change of students
	iii	Attitude change of staff
	iv	Teaching skills
	v	Staff behaviour – code of practice
	vi	Curriculum changes
	i	Whole school policies
	ii	Community education
Institutional Policies	iii	Democratisation of schools
and Wider Alliances	iv	Institutional support for innovations
	v	Local community alliances
	vi	Equal opportunity policies
	i	Recruitment/promotion of black teachers via section 11 via mainstream appointments
Racial Equality for Blacks	ii	Cultural retention within the curriculum
	iii	Other 'special needs' provision
	iv	Parental involvement/consultation
	v	Acceptance of political campaigns as an aspect of education.

Finally, we want to draw attention to those themes which are common to all policies and which, in addition, constitute bridges between the multicultural and antiracist education paradigms. These bridges, or continuities, are both explicit and implicit. Explicitly they can be found in the range of policy goals which we have drawn attention to in this chapter. These show that antiracism is presented as one strategy for achieving multicultural goals. At the implicit level, a careful examination of the policies reveals that certain key words and concepts which figure prominently in antiracist documents simply echo the concerns of the multicultural paradigm. The specific ways in which these terms are deployed shows that there is a considerable overlap in the assumptive bases of these supposedly distinctive approaches. Let us elaborate this argument.

To begin with, stability in schools is seen to be threatened by outside racist groups and by the racialist behaviour of white students. All the Authorities draw attention to the ways in which schools might deal with such incidents. For Brent, racism prevents the development of a cohesive society; it also stops people from co-operating genuinely (Berkshire) and so undermines understanding, tolerance and self-respect. Consequently it will not be tolerated (Bradford). Harmony is another key word and the apparent cornerstone of a truly multicultural society (Haringey). However, it is threatened by black resistance to racism and inequality and unless racism is eliminated, unrest, disorder (Berkshire) and overt disruption (Brent) will follow inevitably. Policymakers in Sheffield recognise that many people believe that differences in outlook, patterns of behaviour and languages will create discord; the imperative must be to re-educate such people.

Justice, as we demonstrated earlier, is taken to mean civil and political rights and greater racial equality. All are necessary to maintain a democracy, according to Brent, and a cohesive society (Berkshire). Those who have no sense of belonging and suffer from a lack of power should be treated as equal citizens and accorded equal rights and opportunities. There is also frequent reference to equality which is always interpreted as equality of opportunity for individual mobility. This will be achieved by liberating talents, changing examinations (ILEA) and improving life chances (Brent). Finally, we come to the truth. This provides an educational rationale for curriculum reforms by challenging the intellectual justification for white superiority and ethnocentrism (Brent) which gives a false view of identity (Berkshire, ILEA). Ignorance is seen as an important basis of discrimination (Brent); thus, it is in the interests of all that truth prevails (ILEA). The term is used to demonstrate an educational rather than a political justification for antiracism and to make explicit the relevance of antiracism in all educational milieux, irrespective of location or the ethnic mix of the student population. In all, therefore, it is clear that the key concepts of antiracist education policies - stability, harmony, justice, equality and the truth - do not constitute a radical break from earlier educational concerns. On the contrary, they have been the staple diet of educational policies for at least the last three decades.

Mullard and his colleagues have argued that: 'the presence of Black groups, and the management of racism constituted the dominant contextualisation from which the production of policy and practice in race and education developed' (1983 et al, p.84). What we have attempted in this chapter is to demonstrate empirically the truth of this claim; to show the various ways in which this occurs, highlight the specificity of local developments and draw attention to the underlying coherence, continuities and commonalities of antiracist policies. We can now provide a more detailed analysis and explanation of these processes and trends.

FOOTNOTES

1. The documents and policies consulted in this and the following chapter are presented below:

BERKSHIRE:

(1) Education for Racial Equality: General Policy Paper (1983).

(2) Education for Racial Equality: Implications (1983).

(3) Education for Racial Equality: Support (1983).

(4) Education for Racial Equality: Paper for Discussion (Advisory Committee for Multicultural Education), (1982).

(5) Education for Equality: Summary Leaflet

BRADFORD:

(1) Local Administrative Memorandum (L.A.M): Schools 13- and 13+ (2/82): Education for a Multicultural Society: Provision for Pupils of Ethnic Minority Communities (1982).

(2) L.A.M. : School 13- and 13+ (6/83): Racialist Behaviour in Schools (1983).

BRENT:

(1) Education for a Multicultural Democracy: Book 1 - 'The Need For a Change From a White Ethnocentric Approach' (1983).

(2) Education for a Multicultural Democracy: Book 2 - 'Analysing Implicit Assumptions on which Current School Practices are Based' (1983).

HARINGEY:

(1) Racialist Activities in Schools (1978).

(2) Educational Aims and Objectives for and in a Multicultural Society (1982).

INNER LONDON EDUCATION AUTHORITY (ILEA):

(1) Race, Sex and Class: 1 – Achievement in Schools (1983).

(2) Race, Sex and Class: 2 – Multiethnic Education (1983).

(3) Race, Sex and Class: 3 – A Policy for Equality – Race (1983).

(4) Race, Sex and Class: 4 – Anti-Racist Statement and Guidelines (1983).

(5) Race, Sex and Class: 5 – Multiethnic Education in Further and Higher Education (1983).

(6) Race, Sex and Class: 6 – A Policy for Equality – Sex (1985)

(7) Aide-Memoire for Inspectorate (1981).

MANCHESTER:

(1) Multicultural Education (1982).

(2) Antiracist Education Policy Statement (Draft for Consultation) (1984).

(3) Institutional Policy on Racism (IPOR) (1982).

(4) Internal Memorandum for Inspectorate on the Development of IPOR (1984).

(5) An Introduction to Multicultural Education in the Primary School (1984).

(6) Reviewing the Secondary Curriculum (1982).

(7) Labour's Policy for Manchester: 1984 Election Address (1984).

SHEFFIELD:

(1) Education in Schools in Multicultural Sheffield (1982).

(2) Curriculum Policy: Education for a Multicultural Society (draft document in response to circular 6/81) (1983).

(3) Education in Multicultural Sheffield (Draft LEA Policy Statement) (1984).

(4) Report from Sheffield CRE: Summary of 3 Meetings to consider draft policy (1984).

(5) Sheffield Ethnic Minorities Unit: Paper on Functions (1983).

2. This determination to ensure general party political support for antiracist policies in Sheffield extends beyond the Education department. In late 1983 the Ethnic Minorities Unit declared that it would develop an all-party policy statement on racism which will have implications for the practices and procedures of all the major departments in the City Council.

Chapter Six

ANTIRACIST EDUCATION POLICIES: A CRITICAL APPRAISAL

Our analysis of the way seven LEAs have racialised their educational policies indicated that despite some important distinctive features, the general conceptualisation of themes and issues could be understood primarily in terms of a common rationale and structure. In this chapter we shall elaborate this argument in the form of a critique of the way these LEAs perceive and respond in policy terms and in their provision to the presence of racial inequalities in the UK.

The purpose of our critique should not be misconstrued. Our main aim is to tease out some of the contradictions and inconsistencies in current policies in an effort to provide some alternative policy options available to LEAs with particular ideological and political commitments. We shall offer these alternatives in our final chapter. But it seems to us that a constructive, critical appraisal of current policies provides the most appropriate basis for the formulation of policies which might be more effective in mitigating racial inequalities in education.

Our critique rests on our understanding of LEAs and individual schools as sites of struggle. They are settings where responses to the state's economic and political policies, established bureaucratic and professional practices, and forms of ethnic mobilisation are negotiated and settled. From this vantage point we would not expect LEA policies necessarily to be coherent, rational or theoretically sophisticated documents. Rather we would expect them to be characterised by contradictions and conflicts. It is the nature of these characteristics we wish to draw attention to and explore and which, in consequence, should permit the emergence of more realistic alternatives.

Naturally, we are not the first critics of the current trend towards racialisation in education policy and provision. Attacks have already been mounted from all points on the political continuum. These deserve some attention if only because they illustrate what writers of different political persuasions understand as the essential features and inevitable consequences of antiracist education policies. They also present a contrast to our own critique.

THE CRITICS: RIGHT, LEFT AND CENTRE:

In March 1984 Anthony Flew, Emeritus Professor of Philosophy at Reading University, published, through the right-wing Centre for Policy Studies, a trenchant critique of what he saw as the 'new and neo-Marxist conception of racism' and 'its implications for education' (1984, p.4). Although concerned with the general racialisation trend in education, Flew was interested particularly in the Berkshire and ILEA policy documents; the latter, in his words, representing 'the full-frontal, hardcore version of Benno-Bolshevism' (1984, p.5). The significance of the distinctive political complexions of these two Authorities is not lost on Flew, as we shall soon see.

The thrust of Flew's criticism is the emphasis in the policy documents on equality of outcome rather than equality of access, the interpretation of 'racial disparities' in educational performance as forms of 'racial inequalities' and the consequent reliance on racism and discrimination, not cultural variation and genetics as explanatory concepts in this process. He asserts that the likely result of the formalisation of such misinterpretations and misconceptions is that: 'we are going sooner or later to be asked to condemn and abandon any and every institution or practice the actual effects of which are that the racial distribution in any social group is substantially different from that in the population as a whole' (1984, p.11). Thus he decries efforts to initiate a 'revolution of destruction against the traditional, colour-blind public education' in Inner London and elsewhere (1984, p.22). But what disturbs Flew above all else is the apparent collusion of Conservative councillors, especially in Berkshire, with this 'neo-Marxist' and 'fallacious' interpretation of events. His document then is meant to assume strategic importance, designed to heighten his political colleagues' awareness of 'Benno-Bolshevism' and prepare them with the means by which they might resist and dissent from the antiracist education movement. As he puts it:

> The point of covering both Berkshire and ILEA is at one and the same time both to bring out the full policy implications of these Radical ideas and to show that no LEA is safe, except in so far as it contains members both willing to resist and properly briefed for the job (1984, p.5).

The criticisms voiced by Raymond Honeyford, the headteacher of Drummond Middle-School in Bradford, have corresponded closely with those of Flew. Writing in The Salisbury Review, 'a quarterly magazine of conservative thought', Honeyford also rejected claims that the relatively poor educational performance of 'West Indian' students was explicable in terms of racism. Instead, 'the roots of black educational failure are in reality located in the West Indian family structure and values, and in the work of misguided radical teachers whose motives are basically political' (1984, p.31). On these grounds Honeyford has embarked on a well-publicised crusade against the LEA's antiracist initiatives, insisting that the imperative should be to encourage (black) immigrants to recognise 'British traditions of civilised discourse and respect for reason' (1984, p.32).

The right-wing critiques of Flew and Honeyford constitute an attempt to deflect political attention away from the structural bases of racial inequality by emphasising pathological explanations for disparities in educational outcomes. We oppose strongly these views; they do, however, allow us to distil the essential features of antiracist education policies. First, the determination to change existing inequalities by focusing on equality of outcome not access. Second, the primacy given to racism not cultural pathology, social engineering not genetics, and cultural equalities not cultural hierarchies as key explanatory variables. What is especially disturbing, however, is that the critiques of Flew and Honeyford - founded on traditional conservative pro-white and meritocratic principles - reasonate closely with many of the other prevailing views on the nature and purpose of education and might therefore facilitate the 'white blacklash' developing in areas such as Bradford and Inner London (Passmore, 1983; Selbourne, 1984).

Robert Jeffcoate has mounted his attack on antiracist education from a 'liberal, egalitarian and integrationist' standpoint (1984b, p.xi). With his erstwhile collaborator, Alan James (1983), Jeffcoate sees antiracism as indoctrination. Thus in James' words, it is inconsistent with an education geared towards fostering 'independent, rational judgements and with openness to the diversity of human thought and behaviour' (1983, p.22). Both Jeffcoate and James maintain that schools should develop 'transcultural' rationality which should subordinate concerns for cultural retention and maintenance.

Jeffcoate argues that antiracists are guilty of obfuscation and illiberalism. On the first point: 'Preoccupation with racism to the exclusion of all else, and with outcomes and effects rather than intentions or causation, goes some way to explaining why anti-racists have so frequently misidentified the nature of the problem to be addressed and been fighting the wrong battle' (1984b, p.147). On the issue of illiberalism, he writes: 'The main reservations to be expressed about anti-racism concern recent initiatives by a few local authorities and schools which appear to threaten the autonomy of teachers and pupils and to evoke the spectres of indoctrination and totalitarianism' (1984b, p.150). His criticisms spring both from a specific form of antimarxism and from a commitment to a version of a child-centred philosophy of education which insists on the neutrality of the teacher and the right of students to express their opinions in the classroom, irrespective of their political and ideological flavour. They also rest on two other highly contentious assumptions. First, that teachers already regard verbal abuse, bullying and graffiti as serious misdemeanours and do not need to be told by politicians and administrators how to deal with these offences when they assume a racist nature. Second, that the present school curricula are truthful and accurate and provide ample scope for antiracism in forms that students want. Now as our earlier discussions show, we are sympathetic to Jeffcoate's misgivings about the use of racism as an all-embracing concept to cover a multitude of sins. However, we disagree profoundly with the assumptive bases of his attack on antiracism. For instance, a recent survey has indicated that some teachers underestimate grossly the explicitly racist nature of some verbal and physical abuse by white students in schools (Troyna and Ball, 1985b). Secondly, Jeffcoate falls into the trap of equating only socialist commitment with indoctrination. We showed earlier that antiracists have responded particularly to the inadequacies of the curriculum; to the untruths, bias and indoctrinating features inherent in most traditional accounts of, say, the British Empire, Imperialism, The Third World and so on. What Jeffcoate fails to emphasise is that in most aspects of contemporary life in the UK political and citizenship rights are not given willingly and rationally; they are being fought for.

Perhaps ironically, antiracist education policies have also attracted criticism from left-wing writers and educationists. Some of this criticism derives from disillusionment with the loose relationship between policy rhetoric and implementation. This is certainly the basis of Amrit Wilson's critique of the ILEA policy (1984). She points out that the antiracist stance taken by the ILEA has been ineffectual in the controversy surrounding the education of NF supporter, Patrick Harrington, at one of the Authority's institutions, the Polytechnic of North London. In the light of these events, Wilson writes that it is difficult to escape the view that the ILEA's policy is based more on political expediency than a genuine commitment to antiracism. These and related critisims were voiced by contributors to the journal, Teaching London Kids, in 1984. There, contributors pointed to the lack of clarity in the ILEA package, the optimistic and unfounded emphasis on the efficacy of equality of opportunity and the failure of policy-makers to outline effective strategies to deal with the problems they specify.

Radical critiques also stem from particular understandings of the relationship between the (national and local) state, the educational system and effective antiracist policies. Here, Natasha Sivanandan dismisses ILEA's antiracist policies as a new form of state control and co-option designed, above all else, to diffuse black struggles through the development of a multiethnic bureaucracy whose role is to divert, protect and socialise a group of compliant Blacks (1984, p.41). Hatcher (1985) is also sceptical of the way antiracist education policies have been formulated. He argues that these policies must be overtly political in their aims and that in the context of the current crisis they must, necessarily, be anti-Tory in their principles and intended practices if they are to be effective.

Earlier chapters should have made clear our sympathy with the lines of argument drawn by Sivanandan, Hatcher and other radical critics. Indeed, we outlined in chapter 1 precisely how the relatively radical notion of mutliculturalism was ultimately appropriated by the state, denuded of its political and educational potential, and transformed into an ideological justification for the perpetuation of racism and racial inequalities. Is it inevitable that antiracism will follow the same trajectory? Currently, there seem to be two possible ways to prevent this happening. The first is to argue for the development of antiracism outside the control of any form of state machinery. This is Mullard's idealised strategy, evident in his insistence that the thrust of antiracism can only be weakened by the state's benediction for and involvement in its promotion (1984). For Mullard, the differences between multiculturalism and antiracism, at the moment at least, are irreconcilable, and highlighted by the distinctive position of their advocates, their policy targets, the nature of alliances and, crucially, their differential relationship to the state.

An alternative response focusses on the forms by which antiracism might be institutionalised within the setting of the local state. What is stressed here is an understanding of the local state as a site of struggle and as a system which is not impervious to penetration and change from below (see Ben-Tovim, et al forthcoming). This is a useful corrective to what may be called the deterministic accounts outlined earlier; so, in the words of Andy Green: 'There is a danger of being too purist on this issue, of believing that anything which the state or progressive sections of the state take up is immediately contaminated' (1982, p.29).

The veracity of these analyses cannot be determined by theory alone. It is particular developments in practice which enable us to assess the radical potential provided by policies for the removal of discriminatory processes and racial inequalities. This is why we need to scrutinise current policy discussions from this perspective. It should allow us to pinpoint the nature of the contradictions and conflicts within policy documents and demonstrate the ways in which they mirror comparable processes in the local state. In all, a detailed, empirical outline of the policies has provided a basis from which we might engage with the wider debates on state power and the reformist potential of particular educational policies.

We are aware, of course, that policy-making entails a number of conflictual processes and, in the words of John Dearlove, the need to take 'trauma-producing decisions' (1973, p.5). As Edelman has put it:

> Governmental rhetoric and action, taken together, comprise an elaborate dialectical structure, reflecting the beliefs, the tensions, and the ambivalences that flow from social inequality and conflicting interests (1977, p.19).

The results of these conflicts, the compromises eventually reached are embodied in the words and phrases of policies. Antiracist policies are, then, negotiated products of academic and political debate about the terms, racism and institutional racism; the selective incorporation of specific demands made by groups who enjoy differential access to power; and particular professional understandings of the purpose of education and its potential as an agent of social and political change. In blunt terms, policies constitute a negotiated settlement - evidence of the way in which conflicts are resolved formally in bureaucratic and political settings. A detailed scrutiny of LEA policy documents allows us to focus on two particular aspects of this process. Firstly, we can tease out the key inferential assumptions and the way these are used to signal how educational problems are defined and located. Secondly, we can draw attention to what is absent from these policies, what issues are never raised and what options are omitted routinely from the policy agenda. This is important if we are to specify how policies prioritise certain interpretations of reality and develop practices and provision on the basis of these interpretations.

'CONDENSATION SYMBOLS':

At the end of chapter 5 we argued that despite variations in content and approach, it was possible to distil five themes which underpinned the way racism was conceptualised and handled in our seven LEAs' policies and documents. These themes were signalled by certain key phrases or concepts, what Edelman has defined as 'condensation symbols'. According to Edelman (1964) these have deliberate political purposes: to create symbolic stereotypes and metaphors which reassure supporters that their interests have been considered. But the symbols have contradictory meanings so that the proposed solutions may also be contradictory or ambiguously related to the way supporters originally view the issue. We wish to demonstrate the ways in which the current presentation of antiracist policies conceals fundamental disputes about the nature, origin and perpetuation of racism and the specific role of education in this process. Unless these arguments are opened up for discussion policies will tend to remain at the level of rhetoric, and cynicism will be reinforced. We can illustrate this argument substantively by looking at the four most obvious 'condensation symbols' in LEA antiracist documents.

(a) Plural society:
We have already noted how in most policy documents the terms, harmony and stability, figure largely. They are also generally associated with the notion of a plural society, or some variant of this such as 'multicultural society'. What is significant here is that the concept is used in policy documents both in a normative and substantive manner; that is to say, there is a recurrent conflation in the use of plural society as both a descriptive and as an ideal prescriptive term is often conflated. The difference, in other words, between what society is and what society should be is obscured.. This ideological sleight of hand allows policy-makers to construct what Bullivant designates as 'specious models of society' (1981, p.228). Consider the following statement found in the first of Brent's booklets: 'The council is committed to a fundamental and significant change to a multicultural education based on a concept of cultural pluralism. The recognition that all people and cultures are inherently equal must be a constant from which all educational practice will develop' (p.5). Or Haringey's claim that the Authority comprises 'a multiracial, multicultural society and the council will continue to foster good relations between all sections of the community ... cultural diversity has enriched, not weakened British society' (1978, p.6). And finally, the assertion made by Sheffield's multicultural support group that: 'Schools need to recognise the growing need to prepare all their youngsters for life as citizens in a just, humane,

multicultural democracy'. In each of these passages it is difficult to distinguish actual descriptions of society from wishful thinking about what society might become.

The political symbolism behind these assertions is that of a harmonious society where divisions based on perceived racial differences are no more or less significant than cultural divisions. This simplistic portrayal of the complex nature of the term culture, allows policy-makers to promote the view that cultural and racial divisions are synonymous; that the subordination of black people in the UK is due as much to their cultural distinctiveness as it is to the fact that they are designated racially inferior. These confusions enable discussion to switch from an outline of existing divisions, conflicts, discrimination and racial inequalities to an ideal which we may all strive towards, with no clear analysis of how the two are related. We are suggesting then that what is represented is a contestation over those features of pluralism which, on the one hand, are seen as politically important and those which, on the other, are of particular concern to the education system. Put simply, policy rhetoric is expressed in terms of political pluralism and hinges on an analysis of the structural features of racial inequalities. Policy proposals, however, focus on cultural pluralism and the ways in which this should be acknowledged and integrated into the educational system. The documents produced in Berkshire and ILEA are the most dramatic exemplars of this shift in that both begin with a structural analysis of racism without clarifying how and in what ways the education system is related to this. The essence of the problem lies in the failure of the policies to distinguish between life styles and life chances; to assume, that is, that education is the determinant of life chances in the UK and is therefore the main source of structural inequalities. What is required in these policies is more emphasis in the initial analysis on the educational system, an acknowledgement of its limited role in the perpetuation of racial inequalities in the UK and a linking passage which paves the way for a focus on specific educational concerns.

(b) Justice:

In policy documents, 'justice' embraces a wide range of citizenship rights; from the right not to be abused physically or verbally because of one's skin colour, ethnic or religious background, to the more ambiguous right to have one's history and culture reflected in a respectable, non-tokenistic manner in the day-to-day routines of the school. Justice signifies the goal of the policies and the provisions they recommend. But when the concept is deconstructed the ambiguities and contradictions which are concealed in its eveyday use are immediately exposed. For instance, because the UK is an unequal society, stratified by race, class and gender, it follows logically that an essential part of natural justice demands an acknowledgment of both acceptable and unacceptable inequalities. Clearly on the basis of Berkshire's pronouncement, racial inequalities are seen to be unacceptable in so far as black students are over-represented in low status positions in school and society. Thus:

'There will be perfect racial justice in Britain if and when the practices, procedures and customs determining the allocation of resources do not discriminate, directly or indirectly, against ethnic minority people and when these practices are on the contrary fair to all' (Berkshire (1), p.5). The policy then goes on to declare that: 'There will be racial justice in education, it follows, if and when the factors determining successful learning in schools do not discriminate, directly or indirectly, against ethnic minority children' (ibid). But, once again, this mystifies rather than clarifies the position. It implies that it is only racial inequalities in society which are unacceptable. It also glosses over the difficult problem of the relationship between different forms of inequality by implying that schools, alone, determine the successful learning of students. Our view is that economic, political, cultural and educational injustices need to be differentiated and the role of the school in perpetuating different forms of injustices has to be acknowledged.

(c) Equality:

It is important to make clear that the term, equality, is used in policy documents as a shorthand term for equality of outcome; that is to say, it embraces the liberal concern of ensuring that equality of opportunity is achieved when 'the proportion of people from different social, economic or ethnic categories at all levels and in all types of education are more or less the same as the proportion of these people in the population at large' (Halsey, 1972, p.8). This ideological and policy standpoint is given full expression in Berkshire's document:

> There will be perfect racial equality in Britain if and when Asian and Afro-Caribbean people participate fully in society and the economy and are therefore proportionately involved in management and government at all levels, and are not disproportionately involved in manual work or in unemployment or under-employment.

> There will be racial equality in education, it follows, if and when Asian and Afro-Caribbean people are proportionately involved in teaching and administration at all levels, in higher and further education, and in streams sets, classes and schools leading to higher and further education (Berkshire (1), p.5).

Through their commitment to this classical liberal interpretation of equality, which is essentially geared to a colour-blind meritocracy, policy-makers have generally distanced themselves from alternative interpretations, especially those which denote forms of affirmative action or positive discrimination. In short, equality does not necessarily mean 'equal opportunities' in this context, a point made clear in Berkshire's General Policy:

> No, the statement is not recommending positive discrimination. That is, it does not envisage that membership of an ethnic

minority could ever be a reason, in itself, for treating one individual more favourably than another (Berkshire (1), p.3).

This is curious because, ostensibly, the main rationale for antiracist policies is precisely to counteract processes whereby membership of an ethnic minority group has historically and currently ensured that some individuals are treated less favourably than others. If this is the case then surely an equal opportunities programme, comprising, at least, affirmative action initiatives, has a part to play?

Equality of outcome, equality of opportunity and racial equality are slogan systems which are used in policy rhetoric to claim legitimacy for reforms. But the nature of society to which these reforms are geared is never specified.

(d) Racism:

The final 'condensation symbol' has already been looked at critically. Suffice it to say that it is often used in policy discourse as a synonym for institutionalised racism to denote how far it has become habituated into routine attitudes, procedures and social patterns. Clearly, however, there is a political dilemma associated with the presentation of policies which take as their starting point the divisiveness of racism. The potential problems this generates tend to be circumvented by the articulation of 'racism' largely in terms of immorality and ignorance rather than oppression and exploitation. Repeatedly the policy focus is on white attitudes towards minority cultures. Thus, changing teacher attitudes via in-service and racism awareness courses constitutes a priority in many LEAs. The 'reformed' teachers are then expected to influence positively their students' racial attitudes. Thus ILEA (2) quotes favourably the following passage from the NUT's Combatting Racialism in Schools: 'Only by adopting such a positive stance (i.e. valuing the cultures and achievements of ethnic minority students) and by using opportunities to replace ignorance with factual information about other cultures and the reasons for immigration to this country, will teachers show that they are effectively anti-racialist' (cited in ILEA (2), p.17). Racism, in other words, can be combatted through a presentation of 'the truth'; that is, a factual, undistorted, objective view of the world. Putting to one side our objections to this oversimplified conception of an antiracist strategy, this discussion of racism generates other, equally problematic issues. If racism is an integral part of a system which historically and currently privileges Whites, then why should Whites be willing to mobilise antiracist initiatives? What would Whites gain, economically, politically or psychologically, from disturbing a system which has served them well? The answer to these questions is found in Berkshire's General Policy: 'Racism is against the long-term self interest of all, since it is bound to lead eventually to social unrest' (p.6). In short, antiracism is a form of pre-emptory strike; an appeal to Whites to concede willingly some of their privileges now in order to prevent those privileges being removed forcibly in the future.

But the passage from Berkshire's policy tells us even more about policy-makers' understanding of racism. To be sure, it is presented as a white problem; nevertheless, antiracism is situated (at least implicitly) in a framework of 'special needs'. Blacks are said to be presenting problems to the educational system through their apparently poor academic performance, disruptive behaviour, demand for supplementary schools and insistence on other specific political concessions. All in all these are seen as examples of their 'special needs' which require 'special treatment' in the form of certain adaptations by Whites to the existing educational system. What is implied then is that in the absence of such 'special treatment' the ideals of social and political cohesion, stability and harmony remain a forlorn hope. The continuities with multicultural approaches are obvious. The strategy comprises the re-education of Whites for harmony and for demonstrating cultural justice to Blacks. Antiracism can be diverted away from a concern with material inequalities towards the removal of barriers which prevent the full flowering of ethnic identities and/or individual social mobility.

What we have done here is to show the potency of 'condensation symbols' in public policy discourse and drawn attention to the various conflicts and contradictions which they at best obscure. Our central point is that through the use of political rhetoric and symbols, policy-makers and their colleagues have failed to engage with fundamental issues which, despite the rhetorical power of policy documents, remain unresolved. We will now illustrate this most clearly by specifying some of the themes and issues excluded routinely from policy agenda and showing how, in the process, certain interpretations assume primacy over others in the formulation of strategies and goals. These omissions can conveniently be divided into theoretical debates and policy recommendations and implementation.

POLICY OMISSIONS: THE THEORETICAL DIMENSION:

(a) Race, class and gender inequalities:
It is ironic, to say the least, that the current debate on antiracism reproduces many of the theoretical weaknesses supposedly associated with multicultural ideologies of educational change. For instance, we have discussed already how policy-makers and others frequently criticised multiculturalism for its emphasis on culture, as distinct from economic location, and for its artificial separation of class from race. In Mullard's terms, the concerns of multicultural education are 'microscopic', those of antiracism, in contrast, are 'periscopic'. Thus: 'Unlike multicultural education which seeks to produce a passive consciousness of cultural differences, anti-racist education seeks to produce an active consciousness of structural similarity, inequality and injustice' (1984, p.33). But what Mullard presents is an ideal scenario, evident in theoretical terms but absent from concrete policy formulations. Mullard's insistence that antiracism 'by definition makes a connection between institutional discriminations, and inequalities of race, class and gender' (1984, p.37), is simply not confirmed by what is contained in antiracist

education policy documents. In the ILEA policy package, for example, three distinctive accounts are provided of differential academic performance along class, gender and ethnic lines. But there is no attempt to cohere them into a unifying and overarching theoretical framework. So how do we account for this omission? Perhaps it is partly due to the academic debates which gave rise to the notions of institutional racism and antiracism; as we have seen, these debates tended to imply not only the primacy but even the autonomy of 'race' as an explanatory concept in the oppression of Blacks. But the separation of class and 'race' may also derive from political considerations. For instance, the definitions of equality and justice which Berkshire policy-makers provide in their General Policy cannot accommodate a class element precisely because they are based on a crude distinction between Blacks and Whites in the UK. Following on from this we can see how by drawing attention to one measure of inequality (i.e. 'race') other forms of inequality (i.e. class, gender) are implicitly taken as acceptable. However, in order to develop policies which will undercut racial inequalities it is necessary to understand 'race' in a class context and consider racism as one of several mechanisms for the reproduction of class position. This cannot be done by a blinkered focus on 'race' alone. Unfortunately, given the particular ideology of equality promoted in LEA policy documents this omission of class is understandable, if regrettable.

There are also theoretical and substantive inconsistencies in the way LEAs engage with the phenomena of gender and 'race' inequalities in education. ILEA (1), for instance, presents data on the academic achievements of girls and Blacks. Unlike the latter, girls are not typified generally as 'educational underachievers' but are shown to perform differentially in certain subjects. The ILEA, therefore, calls for policies which will redirect girls' energies and interest toward more vocationally-oriented, high status subjects such as maths and sciences - areas of the curriculum where traditionally they have performed least well. Significantly, however, and in sharp contrast to theories of black 'educational underachievement', the poor academic performance of girls is seen in the ILEA as a self-volitional response; it is explained in terms which see 'unfemininity' as more threating to their self-image than 'underachievement'. Differences in theoretical explanations are only part of the story however because they lead, directly and indirectly, to distinctive policy recommendations designed to combat the impact of racism and sexism on the academic performance of Blacks and girls.

We have seen how the main thrust of LEA antiracist policies are geared to the eradication of white racism. Logically we might expect ILEA's concern with girls' experiences and performance in school to be translated into attempts to convert all males to an antisexist ideology and set of practices. Indeed, this is referred to in ILEA (6). Nevertheless, we still find that the most important policy recommendations are those in ILEA (1) which are aimed at creating space for single sex groupings in school where girls would be free to develop their own answers and achievements. (One can imagine the reaction to an LEA's proposal that black teachers should be given special responsibility for, say, black maths classes established to prevent unfair competition from white students who, in normal circumstances, receive most of teachers' attention). What is more, the proposed changes in this sphere involve a re-appraisal of mainstream education and a redistribution of mainstream resources. Unfortunately, the absence of any unifying framework in which these differential policy responses might be located and justified prevent us even from speculating on why or how educational policy-makers have reached their decisions on these matters. But when 'race' and gender inequalities are simply highlighted together, as in the development of equal opportunity units and policies, then the lack of clarity in the understanding and policy diagnoses is starkly evident.

(b) The reproduction of racism:

In what senses can it be argued that education is implicated in the generation and reproduction of racism? If racism is a hangover from an imperialist past, simply a contemporary version of scientific racism based on biological and historical ignorance, then an emphasis on re-education as a central strategy is appropriate. But if, as most policy-makers accept, it has contemporary structural roots and is reproduced through existing political, economic and ideological formations, then policies need to engage with these directly, in so far as this is possible within the education system.

Changes in recruitment policies and the allocation of resources, and proscriptions on racist behaviour, are attempts in this direction. But an understanding of racism also needs to confront the issue of why students and teachers are racist. It is obviously inadequate to blame previous monocultural curricula or the lack of black teachers and other professionals for student racism. Surely it would be more relevant to look at the reproduction of racism in the neighbourhood of the school: to ask questions about unemployment, housing conditions, competition, and declining social services, and so discuss racism in the context in which schools experience it. The very brief mention in ILEA (2) of racist organisations benefitting from and exploiting the worsening economic situation is a beginning, but it needs to be extended and made more concretely related to local conditions.

What is missing from most discussions of antiracist curricula is precisely the political nature of such developments. But overt politicisation is not a development which LEAs are willing to legitimate. As Haringey's 1978 document put it: 'The council recognises that politics may quite rightly find a place in a number of courses, but stresses that in curriculum presentation, political bias should always be avoided and teachers should deal with sensitive issues in a mature and balanced way' (1978, p.2). Though it may be difficult for LEAs to endorse party political curriculum developments or for antiracism to be explicitly anti-Tory it is important nevertheless that policy developments allow space for radical and politicised interventions. In his seminal article 'Teaching race', Stuart Hall argued that 'race' is an issue which 'provides one of the most important ways of understanding how this society actually works and how it has arrived where it is' (1980a, p.13). No Authority can dictate that particular ways of understanding this process shall be taught in schools. At this level they can encourage, support and facilitate but must rely on allies among teachers and community groups for pressure and implementation. Further than this they need to respond to suggestions that a central feature of antiracist initiatives should be involvement by educational institutions in political issues of importance to black parents and groups. If racism is largely reproduced outside school then it is necessary to make some links with other struggles at a political level.

Why should (supposedly) radical education policies fail to confront these central issues of racial, class and gender inequalities and the fundamentally political nature of antiracist reforms? Primarily it is because they take for granted the meritocratic purpose of schooling and the role of education as the main distributor of life chances. The policies and provision are directed towards what Brian Salter and Ted Tapper (1981) call a more rational distribution of inequality. As the first of the ILEA's documents makes clear the aim is to improve the attainments of all students and ensure that the 'bottom 40%' does not contain an over-representation of Blacks, girls or students of working class origin. But as we know from the work of Halsey and others, class disparities in educational outcomes have remained remarkably impervious to change. Frances Morrell of the ILEA accepts this but, nevertheless, goes on to assert that the Authority will challenge sexism, racism and classism whenever they arise by looking at the unintentional consequences of actions which lead to less favourable treatment and low expectations of these groups (1984, p.206).

We believe that Ms Morrell's assertion should not go unchallenged. In an education system based on competitive individualism, geared to producing an achievement hierarchy and controlled increasingly by a government which favours a contraction in educational provision and employment opportunities for school leavers, it seems that the shuffling of educational 'haves' and 'have-nots' is neither a possible or desirable aim. Jagdish Gundara (1983) has argued that the central question is not the mobility of Blacks or women in terms of the relative percentage who acquire educational credentials, but the nature of the hierarchy itself. Most policies either explicitly or implicitly endorse existing academic hierarchies and assume direct links between these and occupational and other life chances. An alternative we suggest is to focus more directly upon what education can achieve (even if this is labelled limited and reformist) and, at the same time, to link antiracist strategies with wider equal opportunity policies which have a direct impact on the way the local state distributes its own resources, reappraises its recruitment patterns and allocates its service provision on the basis of social needs. But these comprise explicitly political decisions which involve conflict at the local level and a direct challenge to the monetarist policies of central government. Such issues are, at present, generally seen as beyond the scope of antiracist education policy.

POLICY OMISSIONS: RECOMMENDATIONS AND
IMPLEMENTATION

What stems directly from LEAs' failure to make explicit the
relationship between education and inequality and between the local
and national state is their reluctance to look in any detail at their
own activities and responsibilities. Along with Dorn (1983) we note
that none of the policies deals with the issues of allocation
arrangements, procedures of referral to special education institutions
or units, staffing ratios, expenditure of mainstream budget or
suspension matters. However, each of these plays a major role in the
reproduction of racial inequality and can, by implication, also be
made to work against its perpetuation. In this context, the
differential siting of neighbourhood comprehensive schools (Avon
NUT, 1980; Menter, 1984), the delineation of catchment areas (del
Tufo, et al, 1982) and increased expenditure on disruptive units or 'sin
bins' (Basini, 1981) are important developments which are excluded
from antiracist policy documents.

There is also a tension, if not contradiction between LEAs'
public espousal of antiracism as a policy goal and the recruitment and
operational strategy of specialist teachers who aim ostensibly to
facilitate this objective. As we have seen, the principle of antiracism
rests on the conviction that racism is a white problem and that
efforts must be geared to the re-education of white teachers and
students. To achieve this result all the LEAs in our sample have
appointed specialist advisers/inspectors and created specialist
resource units, funded mainly through Section 11 grants. We pointed
out in chapter 4, however, that the reformulated regulations
governing the allocation of Section 11 money perpetuate the 'special
needs' interpretation associated with multicultural education; in
consequence they both assume and allow for the development of
separate educational institutions and personnel operating within a
distinct professional hierarchy which is funded outside mainsteam
LEA budgets. As Berkshire puts it in its checklist for schools, it aims
to encourage 'the recruitment of ethnic minority teachers' and
therefore asks: 'Is close knowledge and experience of an Asian or
Afro-Caribbean community seen as a positive and relevant
qualification for certain appointments' (Berkshire (2), p.5 Emphasis
added). In all, this suggests that the idea of 'special needs' continues
to be the basis of antiracism. But as John Solomos tells us: 'the
setting up of new agencies to deal with the special problems of black
youth (has become) a way of shunting off important structural
questions into a political siding' (1983, p.16). Of course we recognise
that in times of severe economic stringency and contraction in the
educational system, Section 11 money constitutes an important source
of finance for LEAs. However, there seems to be a case for arguing
that if LEAs are genuinely committed to ensuring that antiracist
principles permeate throughout their local educational institutions
then the reliance on Section 11 funding should be subordinated to a
scrutiny and re-appraisal of mainstream budgets. 'A redistribution of
the existing cake may be more important than trying to make the

cake bigger' if the marginalisation of antiracist education is to be curtailed (Dorn, 1983, p.4).

In each of the seven localities we have looked at, the operational strategies of specialist teachers, the focus and tenor of explicit guidelines and the substantive content of checklists undermine the determination of LEAs to implicate all teachers and students in the institutionalisation of antiracism. In Berkshire's checklist, for example, teachers are alerted to the need to encourage 'bilingual competence', ensure that assessment procedures are 'equally fair and valid for all' and develop ways by which 'ethnic minority parents are fully involved in the decision-making processes which affect their children' (Berkshire (2)). These are all important emphases but they are of little practical assistance to teachers in 'all-white' schools. It is not surprising that teachers, in what are commonly termed the 'white highlands', are often indifferent to calls for multicultural/antiracist education (Troyna and Ball, 1984; 1985b). This was a point picked up by HMI in its document on race relations in schools where it was argued that in such areas 'the immediate experiences of teachers and pupils and the local environment provide few if any pegs on which to hang the work that needs to be done' (1983, p.9). What this comment and our discusssion denotes is that LEA policies comprise few educational justifications for change along antiracist lines, in 'all-white' schools.

The vexed question of how and why antiracist education might relate to the activities and procedures of teachers in 'all-white' schools highlights most vividly the serious omissions from and contradictions in LEA antiracist education policies. They point to ways in which most policy-makers have absolved themselves from responsibility for their own bureaucratic and professional activities, how they have colluded in the marginalisation of antiracism through an almost total reliance on Section 11 finance, and how they have failed to make clear to teachers in the 'white-highlands' ways in which they can develop antiracist pedagogy and strategies. The removal of discrimination and the promotion of racial equality in inner city schools may be more important than any change in suburbia; this is a political decision which councillors and professionals could justify. The point we want to stress is that, at the moment, these same people claim to be developing policies which implicate all schools and which aim primarily at the eradication of white racism. This suggests the need for further intellectual clarification of aims and political honesty regarding priorities and strategies. Both these tasks require a head-on confrontation with existing contradictions rather than symbolic rhetoric. But we must return to our initial theoretical guidelines. LEAs are not independent, all powerful initiators of change. Intellectual clarification is only one process in educational reform and like others is subject to limits imposed by local and national state contexts. It is to these limits and policy options within them that we can now turn.

CONCLUSION

We have been concerned in this book with the changing nature and focus of LEAs' ideological and policy positions on racial matters in education and the ways in which these have been couched and justified in deracialised and racialised discourses. We have seen how the ideology of assimilation, one of the organising principles of the education service in the 1960s and early 70s, has been rejected in a small but growing number of LEAs in favour of a racialised conception of the relationship between educational orientation and provision, and the presence of black students in local schools and colleges. We do not want to exaggerate the extent or influence of this racialised approach in education; nevertheless, it is a development which should not be ignored. According to the Swann Committee this departure from earlier educational paradigms can be attributed largely to the emphasis put on racism as a cause of black 'underachievement' in the interim report of the committee (i.e. the 'Rampton' report) which appeared in 1981. We do not agree with this simplistic and mono-causal explanation. What we would say is that since the early 1980s educationists and others have apprehended more fully the negative influence of racism on the educational experiences and careers of black students and that policies to mitigate racism now figure prominently on the agenda of an increasing number of LEAs. Here we would agree with Swann that:

> Even those people who would challenge its very existence in this country however now seem to accept (racism) as a concept which justifies full and careful consideration and are willing to consider the possibility that certain attitudes and procedures may work against particular ethnic minority groups in society (1985, p.10).

It seems to us that this gradual trend towards racialisation in educational discourse cannot be divorced entirely from changing ideological appraisals of the influences of the school and structural factors in the educational performance of students. As we saw in chapter 1, educationists in the 1960s relied heavily on 'cultural' interpretations of the relatively poor academic performance of Black and working class students. From this vantage point, the black/working class family and its socialisation practices were singled out as the 'villain of the piece'. But as Halsey pointed out in 1974 this interpretation was gradually, if not entirely, eschewed in favour of what he termed 'social' and 'structural' theories of poor performance. The former emphasises the failure of the school to provide relevant educational stimuli to working class and black students and hence contributes to their 'underachievement'. The latter theory recognises that the limited structure of opportunities available to these students in their post-school lives has an influence backwards on their commitment and motivation to succeed in the formal educational setting. There does seem to be a discernible and complementary relationship between these changing interpretations of educational performance and a tentative move in racial ideologies (as they appear in educational policies) from assimilation to antiracism. Once it had been acknowledged that racism, operating in schools and society at large, might have a deleterious effect on the educational experiences and performance of black students, the formulation of policies to mitigate those effects became easier to justify in 'educational' terms.

In the course of tracing these developments we have also noted changing styles of LEA policy intervention which, we have argued, have become increasingly more prescriptive and proscriptive in those Authorities which have racialised their formal policies and approaches. The accompanying diagram is intended to periodise and summarise the various and general developments we have discussed so far (see Diagram 3 p.124).

We began the book by looking at the socio-political and educational context in which multicultural education emerged and achieved respectability in the 1970s. In particular we focussed on why two LEAs, Inner London and Manchester, had opted for multicultural approaches in response to important political and ideological developments nationally and locally. Now we want to examine the relationship of local state options and these developments specifically in relation to the rise of antiracist education. What strikes us as especially interesting is why only a small number of LEAs has developed policies in this direction and why, also, central government has shown virtually no interest in these initiatives. Indeed on this second point we can go even further. Not only has central government shown no interest, but the direction of educational change which it has orchestrated has been in direct opposition to these local policy initiatives. We have seen that these policies emphasise child-centred pedagogies, school-based policy initiatives, local autonomy and a range of other practices which are clearly out of step with central government's overall determination to aggrandise its power over the education system (DES, 1985). This has seen the DES assume a louder voice in decisions affecting the curriculum, examinations, teacher training courses and professional practices; it has also seen the unprecedented involvement of non-educational bodies, such as the Manpower Services Commission (MSC), into educational decision-making. The technical and vocational education initiative (TVE1), for example, did not stem from the educational policy community - indeed that community was not even consulted at the planning stage - but from the MSC (Moon and Richardson, 1984). And as Brian Simon points out, it is this distinctive mode of state interference with the education system, as much as the spurious rationale for interference, which gives cause for concern.

> ...involvement by the state in the restructuring and control of education for social/political purposes has been apparent at least from the middle of the last century and earlier. What is new are the modes of control now being developed and brought into play. Significantly, the state, instead of working through and with other social organisations (specifically local authorities and teachers' organisations) is now very clearly seeking a more direct and unitary system of control than has ever been thought politic - or even politically possible - in the past (1984, p.21)

This perceptible shift in central government's control over educational decision-making has been justified largely on the grounds that schools have not been sufficiently responsive to 'national needs' and therefore require stricter guidance and direction to ensure that there is a greater compatibility between what the student experiences in school and what will be required of her/him in the world of work. As the white paper, Better Schools, declared: 'It is vital that schools should always remember that preparation for working life is one of their principal functions' (1985, p.15). An important corollary of this development has been a declining interest in equality of opportunity both as a fundamental precept and as an organisational strategy of the UK's educational system. This, in turn, has presaged a greater emphasis on selectivity and inequality as witnessed in central government's support for the assisted places scheme, its control over local secondary education reorganisation proposals and the restratification of public examination systems. As Hall observes: 'Inequality in education has become, once again, a positive social programme' (1983, p.3 Original emphasis). It is against this background that the, admittedly slow, growth of local antiracist education policies appears anomalous. After all, these are all linked inextricably to notions of equality of opportunity. It seems to us that this contradictory set of developments requires attention.

'RACE' IN NATIONAL AND LOCAL SETTINGS:

Perhaps it is best to begin an exploration of this dilemma by considering the part assigned to Blacks in the current economic crisis and the implications this has for the educational system. The restructuring of international capitalism both in terms of investment and the division of labour, the consequent decline of British manufacturing and associated growth of 'surplus labour' are matters which we cannot describe in detail here. What is particularly important for our purposes is the way in which 'race' has been entwined with these profound structural changes.

Conclusion

Earlier in the book we noted that black migrants had been encouraged to settle in the UK in the decade and a half following the Second World War. In particular, they were channelled into the low-status, unskilled and semi-skilled jobs vacated by white indigenous workers at a time of economic expansion. But as replacement labour, first and foremost, they were directed not only into specific occupational positions but also towards particular industrial and geographical areas. From the early 1960s, however, the processes of economic restructuring meant that these particular forms of labour were no longer required from the colonies and ex-colonies. What is more, their racial categorisation allowed the state to instigate a series of progressively more restrictive and racially selective immigration laws which, in effect, designated black settlers and their children as second-class citizens in the UK. The passing of the 1981 Nationality Act and the increasing use of insidious and racist internal controls over Blacks in all spheres of life have simply served to reinforce this differential citizenship status. Black workers also continue to occupy positions at the lower echelons of the labour market and because they are locked into declining industries in decaying areas of the country they are also especially vulnerable to redundancy and prolonged unemployment (Brown, 1984). In present - day Britain, then, it is possible to see tendencies toward a segmentation of labour along racial lines. How then do these structural divisions generated nationally and internationally and which are reinforced by ideological designations of groups perceived as racially different, help us to understand antiracist initiatives in the local state?

First and most obviously, the economic costs of the restructuring of industry have been distributed unevenly. They have been experienced primarily in older industrial cities and, more especially, in the inner areas of those cities; it is in these clearly demarcated geographical areas that the newly-emergent 'surplus population' resides (Brown, 1984; Richardson, 1983). Secondly, political and ideological interpretations of how the ending of 'the long boom' might best be managed have important but different geographical consequences. That is to say, political conflicts about the allocative role of the state are more heated where the need for social investment in housing, social services and so on is greatest. Again this tends to be the inner areas of declining industrial cities such as Sheffield, Liverpool, Birmingham and Manchester, and it is here that the most aggressive battles are fought. The decline in student numbers and the government's concern to create an educational system more responsive to the needs of industry have led to what Stuart Hall has called a series of 'regressive educational offensives' (1983, p.2): the closure and amalgamation of schools, reduced entry into the profession from initial training, calls for greater professional accountability linked to pay structures, and so on. Even in this setting, central government insists that there is no necessary tension between national economic efficiency and traditional educational concerns for individual development.

Thirdly and most importantly for our general argument, it is in these inner cities that the significance of 'race' in these processes is experienced most directly. The ideological perception and conception of black students as 'alien', as threats to established social and cultural mores and as unfair competitors for increasingly scarce resources constitute elements of what Barker (1981) terms 'the new racism', and it is in the generation and perpetuation of these ideas that central government has played an important part. However, these ideas contrast sharply with the avowed educational goals of equality of opportunity, integration, harmony and social cohesion. They are also incompatible with the professional and popular meritocratic view of education. But the presence of young blacks in those areas which have suffered most from the recession, and their status as constituent members of the emergent surplus population, places a new and heavier stress on certain schools because, as Rachel Sharp (1984) points out, it is incumbent on these schools to control and contain these students. In short, 'race' has become <u>one</u> way of distinguishing 'surplus labour' from the rest of the economically-active population, the deserving from the undeserving (Fevre, 1984).

What we have argued so far can be summed up like this: the various ideological, political and economic developments we have touched on have generated, or at least reproduced racial inequalities in the UK. As such they constitute part of the conflictual arena in which the education system operates and is compelled to respond. At the local level these responses will be informed and structured by what local politicians, professional administrators, teachers and black and white activists perceive as the most important priorities. And it is the importance of local specificity in this context which prompts us to refer to LEAs as sites of struggle. What is clear is that in certain local areas these priorities are often perceived and interpreted in racial terms and this has led, in consequence, to policy responses which are racialised. From what we have already written it should be obvious why in some areas 'race' has become the lens through which local events and issues, in the present period of crisis and decline, are seen not only by teachers but also by school students. Recent empirical research can be used to underline our arguments. For example, Christopher Husbands (1983) has demonstrated an important relationship between support and sympathy for the NF in certain urban areas and an interpretation of local economic and cultural decline in racial terms. But is is not only adult communities who invoke 'racial' explanations of the crisis. Raymond Cochrane and Michael Billig (1984) found in their study of 2,500 white youths in mainly working-class areas of the West Midlands that about 30 percent supported contemporary UK fascist groups because they had come to understand and explain their limited life-chances not in terms of economic restructuring and decline but in terms of (unfair) racial competition for jobs. For them, unemployment was the burning issue and the problem: too many Blacks. As a result, a policy of enforced repatriation - which is, of course, the most public of the NF and British Movement's policies - seemed eminently attractive. Paul Willis (1983) has made an equally pertinent if slightly different point when he argues that racism is used by white working-class boys to make acceptable and meaningful whole areas of manual labour; for them, racism interlocked with their definitions of masculinity. The point about these research findings is that they show how racism has come to be part of the commonsense understandings of the way many elements of white working-class communities perceive their identities and economic positions. Racism, in other words, is not just a form of cultural ignorance or misunderstanding, as we are often led to believe.

The contexts in which racism is generated and reproduced suggests that however much teachers might wish to see schools as an effective fortress against a hostile environment, this is a naive and forlorn hope. These institutions are not totally immune from the manifest incidents of racism observed and experienced daily outside the school gates. Nor are they places where white students magically suspend racial interpretations of their current and future life chances. In reality these interpretations of their world might lead to racially-demarcated peer groups in school which by their presence and action affirm particular ethnic and cultural identities. They might also lead to peer group cultures of resistance and educational underdevelopment in the form envisaged by Dhondy (1982). Whatever shape or significance they assume it is reasonable to suggest that in the local areas we have been describing teachers are likely to experience racial issues in direct and manifest forms and these experiences have created 'space' for the development of strategies along multicultural and, latterly antiracist lines.

Let us examine the nature of this 'space' more carefully and outline its specific educational features. We want to argue that the economic, ideological and political changes we have noted have been experienced by educationists as crises of legitimacy to which they have to respond. At one level these crises are of a general nature and help to explain the continuities we uncovered between LEAs of quite different shades of political complexion as well as across those operating with multicultural and antiracist conceptions of educational change. But at another level these crises assume specifically local forms and can therefore only be fully apprehended and tackled in the local context. So what are these crises of legitimacy?

The issue of black 'educational underachievement' figures prominently in this scenario. In earlier chapters we noted that this issue had provoked widespread dissatisfaction and criticism of mainstream educational services amongst the UK's black communities. Amongst other things, concern over black 'underachievement', especially amongst those students of Afro-Caribbean origin, led to an exceptional intervention from central government which, in 1979, established a special committee of inquiry 'into the causes of the underachievement of children of West Indian origin in maintained schools' (quoted in Swann, 1985, p.vii). This issue constitutes a crisis of legitimacy precisely because it throws into question the meritocratic credibility of the education system and, implicitly at least, the professional competence of the system and its operatives. If a discernible group of students is seen to be failing, then despite the state's diminishing concern for equality of opportunity, the liberal-democratic view of schooling as a good thing and as a neutral allocator of credentials is thrown into doubt. The second crisis stems from this ideological conception of schooling and the credentials it confers as the principal route of occupational and social mobility. The implicit contract between success in educational and occupational spheres has been exposed as more complex than is often assumed, particularly for black school-leavers. So, whilst credentials continue to have some influence upon employability and lifechances, racism in the selection and recruitment of young labour also plays a major role in black youths' transition from school to work (see Raffe, 1984 and Roberts, 1984 for discussion of these themes).

A third crisis has emerged around the nature of school knowledge, what we might call the pluralist dilemma in education. After all, if different cultures were to be given the same status, validity and credence in the formal curriculum then the whole matter of status - conferring knowledge would be challenged. Cultural relativism does not fit neatly with objective standards and whilst some might agree with Bhikhu Parekh that the education system should release students 'from the confines of the ethnocentric straitjacket' and enable them to 'go out into the world as free from biases and prejudices as possible' (1985, p.22) such emancipatory impulses are not immediately compatible with national trends toward centrally-controlled examinations, a core curriculum, criterion - referencing, emphasis on the development of work-related skills and the enforced absence of political analysis from YTS courses. Simply put, it seems difficult to reconcile demands for cultural retention and promotion with an education system geared progressively more towards centralising vocational skills in the curriculum.

The fourth crisis hinges on the call for education to foster integration and harmony, particularly since the 1981 urban disturbances. This, of course, was the political leitmotif of the Swann Committee's report, Education For All (1985). Again, this goal remains a forlorn hope as teachers are becoming increasingly aware. They are being asked to generate a unifying ideology and ethos precisely at the time they are having to respond to increasing pressure to foster competitive individualism. In a period when rewards are becoming more scarce, the gap between winners and losers is widening, and child-centred pedagogies are being discredited 'Swann's song' seems at best sanguine, at worst cynical. Finally, we come to the issue of citizenship. The state's orchestration of racism, racist organisations and the forms of racial harassment they promote challenge democratic rights and personal freedoms in direct ways in inner city schools. In consequence, they threaten the relative peace, stability and harmony of classrooms, and teachers have to take decisions about how they want to manage or respond to these intrusions. And these are necessarily of a political nature.

These crises of legitimacy illustrate at least some of the ways in which the state's intervention in and interpretation of current economic trends conditions local experiences of these trends. In all, they have challenged many established educational ideologies, assumptions and practices and have defined the parameters in which subsequent political and educational strategies are debated and developed. The relative autonomy of LEAs, however, creates 'space' for the articulation of policies which might assume one of a number of orientations and emphases. Policies might, for instance, embrace liberal notions of multiculturalism and focus on concepts such as 'the truth' and transcultural rationality. These would lead to the development of a depoliticised curriculum. Alternatively, the 'space' might be filled by a range of more radical antiracist initiatives. Whatever the case it is clear that because LEAs are sites of struggle in which local demography, ethnic mobilisation, established political and professional ideologies and teacher organisations each play a greater or lesser role in the determination of policy options, it is impossible to predict how and in what ways this 'space' will be filled. Only an ethnographic study of a particular area could tease out the relative importance of these factors in the determination of policy outcomes. But from our study at least it should be clearer why only a handful of LEAs has chosen antiracism as a policy option; after all, it is only in a small number of areas that the consequences of state policies have combined in the ways we have described. But it is also important to point out that even these policies are formulated in a setting in which control over strategies of implementation is becoming increasingly centralised. Not only are the overall processes of racialisation circumscribed and controlled by the state but, so, too, are the resources necessary for resistance and innovation. Sir Keith Joseph's summary dismissal of Swann's recommendation for a reappraisal of funding procedures for multicultural/antiracist initiatives demonstrates precisely the veracity of our argument.

THE 'RACIALISATION' OF EDUCATIONAL POLICY AND DISCOURSE:

In chapters 1 and 2 we showed how racism could be perpetuated and justified within educational policy and practice through forms of what we called deracialised discourse. We also suggested that given the salience of 'race' in debates and policies outside educational circles, it was unnecessary to refer explicitly to the significance of this issue within educational discussions; 'race' was taken-for-granted in these debates. We then went on to argue that it was in the face of a stubborn resistance to recognise racism as a process impinging on the educational experiences and careers of black students that certain black activists and academics played a major part in racialising the debate; ensuring, in other words, that the notion of institutional racism became a matter for debate on the educational agenda. This we termed benign racialisation. However, our analysis of LEA policies within this paradigm leads us to believe that they are sharing some of the assumptions which they purport to attack; or, at least, they do not challenge forms of racism as effectively as their authors might lead us to believe. Given that LEAs occupy a terrain which is not entirely of their own choice these constraints and contradictions are not particularly surprising.

Without wishing to appear overtly cynical it seems to us that there is a thin line between demands for cultural retention as a basic citizenship right on the one hand, and a perception of those demands as the 'special needs' of an 'alien' population, on the other. The ongoing controversy about the regulations governing the use of Section 11 grants illustrates this point well, for it is in line with the state's definition of a racialised strategy that the 1982 guidelines for Section 11 grants specified the separate cultural needs of immigrants as the justificatory grounds. Now because central government controls the Section 11 purse strings LEAs have to adhere to these guidelines though they justify their allocation and distribution in terms of a benign racialised policy. This has led to two disturbing developments. First, it has faciliated the emergence of a separate hierarchy of specialisms which are ethnic-specific and justified in terms of the unique cultural competences arising from membership of a particular ethnic group. Secondly, it has led to the allocation of resources to particular ethnic groups in recognition of their 'special needs'. As Paul Stubbs has argued, this has resulted in the development of an 'ethnically sensitive' service which is situated in a special needs paradigm and which justifies cultural competences only as a form of social control. As Stubbs puts it, Blacks are almost compelled to become 'cultural experts' on terms which are dictated by white professionals (1984, p.18). The controversy in Birmingham in 1985 over a special management course for black teachers, on the grounds that they were underperforming professionally, provides a practical illustration of this dilemma.

It is not our task to resolve these matters; rather it is consistent with our general analysis that we present the contradictions and conflicts associated with current educational debates. After all, many black professionals support the priority assigned to 'race' over other forms of oppression and accept as legitimate this rationale for the substitution of Blacks for Whites in the provision of services for black clients. Other commentators, such as Gus John (1981) and Marian Fitzgerald (1984), share our reservations about the practical forms which benign racialisation has assumed. In Fitzgerald's words:

> Among many champions of racial equality there is a tendency to see black people as a homogenous mass and implicitly assume that they are so different from any other group in society that the standard variables do not apply to them. With the exception that the stereotypes this creates are benign rather than malign, this differs little from the racist approach (1984, pp.53-54).

A rather different consequence arising from forms of benign racialisation was discussed in chapters 3 and 4; namely, the tendency to use racism and institutional racism as blanket, undifferentiated terms for an array of very different situations, practices and processes. This has also allowed for the development of policies which ostensibly attack racial inequality but, in fact, may reinforce it. We are thinking especially of moves to integrate discussions of, say, racism, in the curriculum. Of course the way in which this is dealt with will vary enormously from school to school and teacher to teacher. But there is a danger that it may be presented as a cultural or individual phenomenon, dislocated entirely from the structural context in which it is generated and sustained.

The limited understanding of racism in the Swann report, and the naive policy recommendations which it gave rise to exemplifies our concerns (Swann, 1985, p.27 and p. 466). What we have stressed before is the need for a more subtle and differentiated understanding of both 'institutional racism' and 'racism' and a more perceptive, critical appreciation of the various and complex ways in which these phenomena operate in everyday life.

WHAT FORM OF ANTIRACISM?

This leads us, logically, into a discussion of the different policy options available to those genuinely committed to antiracist policies and strategies. What our analysis has highlighted, perhaps above all else, is that the way educationists and policy-makers conceptualise the notion of racism and the relationship between racial inequalities and state power has profound implications for the nature and orientation of LEA policies, and for the strategies they recommend. At the risk of oversimplification, there seem to be three dominant approaches to this complex issue. First there is the approach epitomised by the arguments and strategies outlined in the Swann report. There we are led to believe two things. To begin with, racism is seen to constitute little more than ignorance and misunderstanding about the lifestyles and cultural values of ethnic minority communities. We are told that it is neither a uniquely British phenomenon or a problem peculiar to 'whites' (1985, p.27). From this perspective, in which racism is synonymous with prejudice, the role of education must be 'to equip a pupil with knowledge and understanding in place of ignorance' (1985, p.13). 'Swann's song' leads us to believe, secondly, that the state is neutral and open to rational arguments about the need for multicultural/antiracist education. The imperative then, is to persuade different sections of the state of the political and, more importantly, educational efficacy of this new orthodoxy and provide the technical means through which the goal of 'Education for All' might be achieved. In the words of the Committee: 'countering racism within society at large must be a matter for the Law, for Government, Local Authorities, Employers, Trade Unions, the Commission for Racial Equality, and indeed many others, individually and collectively' (1985, pp.87-88). The ideological conception of the state as responsive to calls for multicultural/antiracist education, racial equality and social and political cohesion, leads the Committee into rejecting calls from the black communities for separate schooling; such a development, we are told, 'would be unlikely to offer equality of justice to the members of all groups, least of all the numerically smaller minorities' (1985, p.5).

A contrasting set of assumptions underpins the views of many radical interpreters of racism. For them, the ideology of racism and the inequalities which it generates are so widespread and fundamental to state power that collusion with the state in the development of antiracist policies and strategies is summarily rejected. In the words of Gus John:

> To wish to integrate with that which alienates and destroys you, rendering you less than a person, is madness. To accept the challenge to join it and change it from within when it refuses to accept that you are there in your fullness and refuses to acknowledge the results of interaction between you and it, is double madness (quoted in Mullard, 1982, p.28).

From this vantage point, the struggle against racism can only be viable and effective when it is mounted in isolation from state agencies. In specific terms, this leads to the setting up of supplementary schools and forms of community education which provide students with the understanding and skills which they will find necessary in the fight for their rights.

A third approach eschews a view of the state as necessarily and inevitably racist in all its spheres. Although there are several distinctive theoretical orientations within this approach there are, nevertheless, two particular emphases which provide a basis for change and reform. First is the conception of an 'extended' or 'integral' state which in the words of Ben-Tovim and his colleagues comprises 'both formal institutions, made up principally of central and local governments and their administrative apparatuses, and informal or private institutions, including those representing industrial and financial sectors of the economy, trade union, political parties, voluntary organisations and so on' (1982, p.307).

A second feature here is the emphasis on struggle: the mobilisation of particular forces to oppose the dominance of the central state, influence forms of resistance and generate alternative policies. The purpose of this approach, then, is to include within the notion of the state arenas of struggle which are conventionally conceived to be outside its boundaries. This conception, therefore, breaks down the state/mass dichotomy which often characterises the literature. We do not want here to engage either in semantic arguments about definitions or in the more detailed theoretical debates which these concepts have generated. Their usefulness depends in part upon the contexts in which they are applied. In the context of a comparative study of local state policies at one particular conjuncture, this notion of the integral state provide a basis for understanding local conflicts and compromises. Particularly useful has been the conceptualisation of contradictions and conflicts as: 'arenas of struggle, contestation and points of potential change and democratisation, rather than as inherently ineffectual or agencies of co- option and diversion' (Ben Tovim et al, 1981 p.168).

We want to stress, however, that we have accepted this approach with certain caveats. The most important of these is a recognition of how the dominance of the central state determines the conditions of both local state autonomy and the range of options available. We have attempted to outline the parameters of this dominance in education and some of its specific consequences.

Secondly, though we accept that political and professional groups in different local contexts will hold different ideologies and establish different alliances, this does not lead us to a pluralistic understanding of local policy processes. Structural and ideological determinations of power and issues provide the limits within which the local scene is played out. Again we have attempted to demonstrate how understandings of professionalism or a particular growth in youth unemployment, for example, intertwine with local politics. Finally we accept that we are focusing only upon intermediate reforms of a limited nature. It is a political decision for those concerned with these struggles whether these limited options provide a radical potential (and the conditions for further antiracist advances), or whether they are of a tokenistic, even harmful nature which might inhibit the success of other struggles.

If the notion of the 'extended' state provides us with the terrain on which the antiracist struggle might be fought it does not necessarily define the form or strategy of the struggle. Once again this hinges on coneptualisations of racism and as we saw in an earlier chapter academics (and others) are far from united on this. For some, racism constitutes an autonomous and analytically independent form of oppression; others prefer an interpretation in which the subordination of Blacks continues to be understood primarily in terms of class positions. Different again is the view of racism as one form of oppression which interlocks with class and gender inequalities and which cannot be tackled effectively independently from those forms (see Brittan and Maynard, 1984 for discussion). These theoretical disagreements are reflected and reproduced in local policies. As we have seen some policy-makers have isolated racial inequality as the evil to be attacked while others, such as those in Liverpool, prefer to mount their attack on inequalities from a class perspective. Interestingly our interviews with Labour party councillors indicated that these disputes were illustrative of basic divisions within the party and signified broader right/left, 'soft/hard' allegiances. But even if we accept Paul Stubbs' (1984) claim that there has been too great an emphasis on the specificity of racial oppression at the expense of a class perspective there are still at least three strategies which would link the range of inequalities within an overall policy. The first would be to follow the example of policy-makers in Liverpool in which class constitutes the defining characteristics of policies but where a range of other oppressions would be subsumed within this framework.

A second strategy would rest on a centralisation of the notion of deprivation and the development of policies geared towards a range of deprived groups. Again, our interviews indicated that this was a popular way of linking the perceived educational needs of 'racial minority' groups with girls and working class students. From this perspective, the effects of teacher expectations and stereotyping and the 'reality' of educational underachievement are defined as experiences common to all these students. This is clearly the ILEA approach for when Frances Morrell writes of attempts 'to identify policies that are likely to change the current patterns of achievement within inner city schools' she is simply adding the perceived effects of classism to those of racism and sexism (1984, p.200 Original emphasis). The third, and arguably the most popular approach, would be to link the struggles of different groups whilst acknowledging in the development of strategies the specific problems confronted by individual constituent groups. The focus here is on wider forms of oppression rather than deprivation: Blacks, women, gays and the handicapped form discrete but component groups within a more general equal opportunities strategy.

This third strategy comes closest to our own theoretical formulation. Predicated on an acceptance of a notion of the 'extended' state and the mobilisation of struggles across different alliances we would support broadly conceived equal opportunity strategies which embraced but did not subsume either the specificities of racial oppression or the autonomy of campaigns specifically against forms of racism. The overall aims of the resultant policy would, of course, extend beyond the education system or at least beyond the narrow way in which 'education' is traditionally conceived. It would comprise a concern for curriculum reform and whole school policies but would also consider recruitment processes and promotion prospects for Blacks, the allocation of money (i.e. grants to local groups, supplementary schools etc.), political campaigns against, say, deportations, service delivery (in the form of school allocations, catchment areas, resources, special educational provision and suspensions) and the democratisation of established forms of decision-making and consultation procedures. It might also be geared to the setting up of community schools as an organisational form which would be responsive to local needs and which would include antiracism amongst a range of community concerns.

Our support for antiracist policies within more broadly based equal opportunities strategies rests on two fundamental convictions. First, that racial inequalities are inextricably linked with and reproduced in conjunction with a range of other oppressions in society, especially class and gender forms. The theoretical dislocation of racism from these other forms does not, in our view, facilitate the development of policies with any reasonable chance of mitigating either its incidence or effects. What we are saying then is that racism has to be adequately contextualised and this compels an analysis of the complex totality in which it functions. This is a point argued forcibly by Hall:

> At the economic level, it is clear that race must be given its distinctive and "relatively autonomous" effectivity, as a distinctive feature. This does not mean that the economic is sufficient to found an explanation of how these relations concretely function. One needs to know how different racial and ethnic groups were inserted historically, and the relations which have tended to erode and transform, or to preserve these distinctions through time - not simply as residues and traces of previous modes, but as active structuring principles of the present society. Racial categories alone will not provide or explain these (1980b, p.339).

Second, we are committed to the view antiracists need to form wider alliances with other political organisations and groups and be involved in wider campaigns if the inequalities they have identified are to be tackled effectively. As Hatcher (1985) suggests, these alliances might implicate antiracists in anti-Tory attacks on monetarism, orchestrated locally, or national alliances between Blacks, sections of the Labour party, trade unions and the women's movement. As we have already indicated, we are not convinced that educational change along the lines we have proposed will emerge from policies which conceive of the state as benevolent, rational and open to conversion. Contrary to the ideological stance assumed both by policy-makers in the areas we have looked at and by the Swann Committee we do not believe that the state is committed to the belief that fighting racism is in the interests of all.

Our approach, even in skeletal form, leaves a number of questions unresolved not least the fact that it is not immediately appropriate for those students in all-white schools or areas. Antiracist strategies for such localities are important for as Bill Taylor reminds us: 'The majority of Britain's population... does not live in inner cities, nor is it in regular contact with non-white people' (1984-5, p.1). Nor, we suspect, would parents and teachers readily accept a political understanding of racism which presented it as integral to the reproduction of other inequalities in the UK and as a way of interpreting the nature and distribution of power in society. In the absence of local pressure from unions, political parties, black groups and activists in such areas perhaps the only way forward is for national campaigning organisations and Trade Unions (such as the NUT, NATFHE and NAME) to mobilise local struggles in these areas. They need to include political and professional understandings of racism. They must stress that educated citizens do not taunt visiting black footballers; they do not accept and reproduce stereotypes, and they do not, most importantly, support or encourage discriminatory laws and behaviour.

The complexity of the task is foreboding: how to provide antiracist education in multi-racist Britain. Clearly it is important to tackle racial inequalities and racism as structural features of society at the same time as developing education policies; as Miles (1984) rightly points out any future government which is genuinely committed to antiracism must emphasise the economic and political regeneration of urban areas. But even if approaches were developed along these lines there is no guarantee that racial inequalities would be significantly challenged. In the end, strategies at many different levels are essential and the widening of focus to equal opportunity policies critical if alliances are to be forged and support secured. The local state is one context in which such developments are now taking place. But racism also has to be understood in the national context. Only from this perspective can we understand fully the complex ways in which 'race', class and gender interlock to reproduce specific forms of racism and racial inequalities.

Diagram 3: The Ideological and Policy Response to Racial Matters in Education

	Racial Ideology [1]	Form (a) [2]	Form (b) [3]	Educational Ideology [4]	Style of Intervention (LEA relationships with schools) [5]
1950s–mid 1960s	Assimilation			Cultural Deprivation	Disinterest
Late 1960s –early 1970s	Integration	Racially Inexplicit	Deracialised	Cultural/ Social	Permissive/ Laissez-faire
Mid-late 1970s	Cultural Pluralism/ Multiculturalism	Racially Explicit			
Early– mid '80s	Antiracism		Racialised	Social/ Structural	Interventionist

1. See the work of Bolton (1979); Mullard (1982); Troyna (1982)
2. Kirp (1979)
3. Reeves (1983)
4. Halsey (1974)
5. Troyna and Ball (1985a)

BIBLIOGRAPHY

Ahier, J and Flude, M (eds.), (1983) Contemporary Education Policy, Croom Helm, Beckenham

Allen, R. (1969) Black Awakening in Capitalist America, Doubleday, New York

Allen, S (1973) 'The Institutionalisation of Racism', Race, 15, July, 99-105

ALTARF, (1980) Teaching and Racism, All London Teachers Against Racism and Fascism, London

ALTARF, (1984) Challenging Racism, All London Teachers Against Racism and Fascism, London

Avon NUT (1980) After the Fire: Education in St Paul's, Avon County Division of the NUT, Bristol

Bachrach, P and Baratz, M S (1962) 'The Two Faces of Power', American Political Science Review, 56, 947-952

Bagley, C (1973) 'The Education of Immigrant Children: A Review of Problems and Policies in Education', Journal of Social Policy, 2, 4, 303-314

Banton, M (1977) The Idea of Race, Tavistock, London

Banton, M (1983) 'Race, Prejudice and Education: Changing Approaches', New Community, 10, 3, 373-380

Baratz, S S and Baratz, J C (1970) 'Early Childhood Intervention: the Social Science Base of Institutional Racism', Harvard Educational Review, 40, 1, 29-50

Barker, M (1981) The New Racism, Junction Books, London

Baron, H M (1969) 'The Web of Urban Racism' in L L Knowles and K Prewitt (eds.), Institutional Racism in America, Prentice Hall, Englewood Cliffs, pp. 134-176

Baron, S et al (1981) Unpopular Education, Hutchinson, London

Basini, A (1981) 'Urban Schools and "Disruptive Pupils" ; A Study of Some ILEA Support Units', Educational Review, 33, 3, 191-206

Benokraitis, N and Feagin, J (1974) Institutional Racism: A Critical Assessment of the Literature and Suggestions for Extending the Perspective, Unpublished, University of Texas

Ben-Tovim, G (1978), 'The Struggle Against Racism: Theoretical and Strategic Perspectives', Marxism Today, July, 203-213

125

Ben-Tovim, G et al (1982) 'A Political Analysis of Race in the 1980s' in C Husband (ed.), 'Race' in Britain: Continuity and Change, Hutchinson, London, pp.303-316

Ben-Tovim, G. et al (forthcoming) 'A Political Analysis of Local Struggles for Racial Equality' in J. Rex and D. Mason (eds.) Theories of Race and Ethnic Relations, Cambridge University Press, Cambridge

Blauner, R (1972) Racial Oppression in America, Harper and Row, New York

Bloom, B, Davis, A and Hess, R (1965), Compensatory Education for Cultural Deprivation, Holt, Rinehart and Winston, New York

Bolton, E (1979) 'Education in a Multiracial Society', Trends in Education, no.4, 3-7

Bowker, G (1968) The Education of Coloured Immigrants, Longmans, London

Briault, E (1973) An Education Service for the Whole Community, Inner London Education Authority, London

Brittan, A and Maynard, M (1984) Sexism, Racism and Oppression, Basil Blackwell, Oxford

Brooksbank, K (1980) Educational Administration, Councils and Education Press, London

Brown, C (1984) Black and White Britain: The Third PSI Survey, Heinemann Education Books, London

Bullivant, B (1981) The Pluralist Dilemma in Education, Allen and Unwin, Sydney

Carby, H V (1982) 'Schooling in Bablylon' in CCCS, The Empire Strikes Back, Hutchinson, London, pp.183-211

Carmichael, S and Hamilton, C V (1967) Black Power, Penguin, Harmondsworth

Child, D and Paddon, M (1984) 'Sheffield: Steelyard Blues', Marxism Today, July, 18-22

Clark, N (1982) 'Dachwyng Saturday School' in A Ohri, B Manning and P Curno (eds.), Community Work and Racism, Routledge and Kegan Paul, London, pp.121-127

Coard, B (1971) How the West Indian Child is Made Educationally Subnormal in the British School System, New Beacon Books, London

Cochrane, R and Billig, M (1984) 'I'm not National Front Myself, But...', New Society, 17 May, 255-258

Commission for Racial Equality, (1984) Monitoring an Equal Opportunity Policy: A Guide For Employers, (Third Edition), Commission for Racial Equality, London

Committee of Inquiry into the Education of Children from Ethnic Minority Groups (Rampton Committee), (1981) West Indian Children in Our Schools (Interim Report) (Cmnd. 8723), HMSO, London

Committee of Inquiry into the Education of Children from Ethnic Minority Groups (Swann Committee), (1985) Education for All, (Cmnd, 9453), HMSO, London

Commonwealth Immigrants Advisory Council (1964) Second Report (Cmnd, 2266), HMSO, London

Community Relations Commission (1974) Unemployment and Homelessness, Community Relations Commission, London

Cox, O C (1970) Caste, Class and Race, Monthly Review, New York

Dale, R et al (1981) Education and the State, Milton Keynes, The Open University (OU, E353)

Daniel, W W (1968) Racial Discrimination in England, Penguin, Harmondsworth

Dearlove, J (1973) The Politics of Policy in Local Government, Cambridge University Press, Cambridge

Department of Education and Science (1965) The Education of Immigrants (Circular 7/65), DES, London

Department of Education and Science (1971) The Education of Immigrants (Education Survey No. 13), DES, London

Department of Education and Science (1977) Education in Schools: A Consultative Document (Green Paper Cmnd. 6869), HMSO, London

Department of Education and Science (1985) Better Schools (White Paper 9469), HMSO, London

Dhondy, F (1982) 'The Black Explosion in British Schools' in F Dhondy, B Beese and L Hassan, The Black Explosion in British Schools, Race Today Publications, London, pp. 43-52

Dorn, A (1983) 'LEA Policies on Multi-Racial Education', Multi-Ethnic Education Review, 2, 2, 3-5

Dorn, A and Troyna, B (1982) 'Multiracial Education and the Politics of Decision-Making', Oxford Review of Education, 8, 2, 175-185

Driver, G (1980) Beyond Underachievement, Commission for Racial Equality, London

Dummett, A (1973) A Portrait of English Racism, Harmondsworth, Penguin

Edelman, M (1964) The Symbolic Uses of Politics, University of Illinois Press, Urbana

Edelman, M (1977) Political Language: Words that Succeed and Policies that Fail, Academic Press, New York

Edwards, V K (1979) The West Indian Language Issue in British Schools, Routledge and Kegan Paul, London

Fenton, S (1982) 'Multi-Something Education', New Community, 10, 1, 57-63

Fenwick, K and McBride, P (1981) The Government of Education, Martin Robertson, Oxford

Fevre, R (1984) Cheap Labour and Racial Discrimination, Gower, Aldershot

Fitzgerald, M (1984) Political Parties and Black People, Runneymede Trust, London

Flett, H (1981) 'The Politics of Dispersal in Birmingham', Working Papers on Ethnic Relations, No. 14, Research Unit on Ethnic Relations, Aston University, Birmingham

Flew, A (1984) Education, Race and Revolution, Centre for Policy Studies, London

Flude, M (1974) 'Sociological Accounts of Differential Educational Attainment' in M Flude and J Ahier (eds.), Educability, Schools and Ideology, Croom Helm, London, pp. 15-52

Foster-Carter, O (1985) 'Racism and the Schooling Crisis in Bradford', Critical Social Policy, No. 12, 69-78

Franklin, R S and Resnik, S (1973) Political Economy of Racism, Holt, Rinehart and Winston, New York

Gabriel, J and Ben-Tovim, G (1978) 'Marxism and the Concept of Racism', Economy and Society, 7, 2, 118-154

German, R A (1983) 'The Commission for Racial Equality and Anti-racist Teaching,' paper presented to the conference, Geography and Education for a Multicultural Society: Context and Curriculum, London, University Institute of Education, 29 March

Gibson, M (1976) 'Approaches to Multicultural Education in the United States: Some Concepts and Assumptions', Anthropology and Education Quarterly, 7, 4, 7-18

Giles, R (1977) The West Indian Experience in British Schools, Heinemann Educational Books, London

Gill, D (1982) Assessment in a Multicultural Society: Schools Council Report: Geography, Unpublished

Gilroy, P (1982) 'Police and Thieves' in CCCS, The Empire Strikes Back, Hutchinson, London, pp. 143-182

Giroux, H (1983) 'Theories of Reproduction and Resistance in the New Sociology of Education: A Critical Analysis', Harvard Educational Review, 55, 3, 257-295

Giroux, H (1984) 'Ideology, Agency and the Process of Schooling' in L Barton and S Walker (eds.), Social Crisis and Educational Research, Croom Helm, Beckenham, pp. 306-334

Gordon, P (1985) Policing Immigration: Britain's Internal Controls, Pluto Press, London

Grace, G (1984) 'Urban Education: Policy Science or Critical Scholarship' in G Grace (ed.), Education and the City, Routledge and Kegan Paul, London, pp.3-59

Green, A (1982) 'In Defence of Anti-racist Teaching', Multiracial Education, 10, 2, 19-35

Gundara, J (1983) 'The Social and Political Context: Education for a Multicultural Society', paper presented to the conference, Geography and Education for a Multicultural Society: Context and Curriculum, London, University Institute of Education, 29 March

Gurnah, A (1984) 'The Politics of Racism Awareness Training', Critical Social Policy, No. 11, 6-20

Hall, S (1980a) 'Teaching Race', Multiracial Education, 9, 1. 3-13

Hall, S (1980b) 'Racism, Articulation and Societies Structured in Dominance' in UNESCO, Sociological Theories: Race and Colonialism, UNESCO, Paris, pp.305-345

Hall, S (1983) 'Education in Crisis' in A M Wolpe and J Donald (eds.) Is There Anyone Here From Education?, Pluto Press, London pp.2-10

Hall, S et al (1978) Policing The Crisis, Macmillan, London

Halsey, A H (1972) 'Political Ends and Educational Means' in A H Halsey (ed.) Educational Priority (Vol. 1), HMSO, London, pp. 3-12

Halsey, A H (1974) 'Government Against Poverty in School and Community' in D Weddeburn (ed.) Poverty, Inequality and Class Structure, Cambridge University Press, Cambridge, pp. 123-139

Hargreaves, A. (1983) 'The Politics of Administrative Convenience - The Case of Middle Schools' in J. Ahier and M. Flude (eds.), Contemporary Education Policy, Croom Helm, Beckenham, pp.23-57

Hargreaves, D (1984) Improving Secondary Schools, Inner London Education Authority, London

Hassan, L and Beese, B (1981) 'Who's Educating Whom?' in F Dhondy, B Beese and L Hassan, The Black Explosion in British Schools, Race Today Publications, London, pp.21-35

Hatcher, R (1985), 'On "Education for Racial Equality" ', Multiracial Education, 13, 1, 30-46

Hatcher, R and Shallice, J (1983) 'The Politics of Anti-Racist Education', Multiracial Education, 12, 1, 3-21

Her Majesty's Inspectorate (1983) Race Relations in Schools: A Summary of Discussions and Meetings in Five LEAs, Department of Education and Science, London

Hodges, L (1978) 'Off to a Prejudiced Start?,' The Times Educational Supplement, 24 February, 10-11

Home Office (1974) Educational Disadvantage and the Educational Needs of Immigrants, (Cmnd. 5720), HMSO, London

Home Office (1978) The West Indian Community: Observations on the Report of the Select Committee on Race Relations and Immigration, (Cmnd, 7186), HMSO, London

Honeyford, R (1984) 'Education and Race: an Alternative View', The Salisbury Review, Winter, 30-32

House of Commons (1981) Fifth Report from the Home Affairs Committee Session 1980-1981: Racial Disadvantage (Vol 1), HMSO, London

Humphrey, D and John, G (1971) Because They're Black, Penguin, Harmondsworth

Husbands, C (1983) Racial Exclusionism and the City: The Urban Support for the National Front, Allen and Unwin, London

Institute of Race Relations (1980) 'Anti-racist not Multiracial Education: IRR Statement to the Rampton Committee on Education', Race and Class, 22, 1, 81-83

Institute of Race Relations (1982) Roots of Racism, Institute of Race Relations, London

James, A (1983), 'What's Wrong with Multicultural Education?,' New Community, 10, 2, 225-231

Jeffcoate, R (1984a) 'Ideologies and Multicultural Education' in M Craft (ed.) Education and Cultural Pluralism, The Falmer Press, Sussex, pp.161-187

Jeffcoate, R (1984b) Ethnic Minorities and Education, Harper and Row, London

John, G (1981) In the Service of Black Youth: A Study of the Political Culture of Youth and Community Work with Black People in English Cities, National Association of Youth Clubs, Leicester

Jones, C and Kimberley, K (1982) 'Educational Responses to Racism' in J Tierney (ed.), Race, Migration and Schooling, Holt, Rinehart and Winston, London, pp. 134-161

Jones, J M (1972) Prejudice and Racism, New York, Addison Wesley

Jones, K (1983) Beyond Progressive Education, Macmillan, London

Joshua, H and Wallace, T (1984) To Ride The Storm, Heinemann Educational Books, London

Katz, J (1978) White Awareness: Handbook for Anti-Racism Training, University of Oklahoma Press, Oklahoma

Killian, L (1979) 'School Bussing in Britain: Policies and Perceptions', Harvard Educational Review, 49, 2, 185-206

Kirp, D (1979) Doing Good by Doing Little, University of California Press, London

Kirp, D (1982) Just Schools, University of California Press, London

Knowles, L L and Prewitt, K (eds.) (1969), Institutional Racism in America, Prentice Hall, Englewood Cliffs

Kogan, M (1975) Dispersal in the Ealing Local Education Authority: A Report Prepared for the Race Relations Board, Unpublished

Kushnick, L (1982) 'Parameters of British and American Racism', Race and Class, 23, 2/3, 187-206

Little, A (1975) 'The Educational Achievement of Ethnic Minority Children in London Schools' in G K Verma and C Bagley (eds.) Race and Education Across Cultures, Heinemann Educational Books, London, pp.48-69

Little, A and Willey, R (1981) Multi-ethnic Education: The Way Forward (Schools Council Pamphlet No. 18), Schools Council, London

Lukes, S (1974) Power: A Radical View, Macmillan Studies in Sociology, London

Mabey, C (1981) 'Black British Literacy', Educational Research, 23, 2, 83-95

Marable, M (1984) Race, Reform and Rebellion: The Second Reconstruction in Black America, 1945-1982, Macmillan, London

Menter, I (1984) 'Multicultural Education: Avon's Calling?' Multiracial Education, 12, 2, 8-14

Merseyside Socialist Research Group (1980) Merseyside in Crisis, Manchester Free Press, Manchester

Miles, R (1982) Racism and Migrant Labour, Routledge and Kegan Paul, London

Miles, R (1984) 'Racialization' in E E Cashmore (ed.) Dictionary of Race and Ethnic Relations, Routledge and Kegan Paul, London, pp. 223-225

Milner, D (1983) Children and Race Ten Years On, Ward Lock, London

Moodley, K (1983) 'Canadian Multiculturalism as Ideology', Ethnic and Racial Studies, 6, 3, 320-331

Moon, J and Richardson, J J (1984) 'Policy-Making With a Difference? The Technical and Vocational Education Initiative', Public Administration, 62, Spring, 23-33

Morrell, F (1984) 'Policy for Schools in Inner London' in G Grace (ed.) Education and the City, Routledge and Kegan Paul, London, pp. 195-209

Morris, G, Hussain, A and Aura, T G (1984) 'Schooling Crisis in Bradford', Race Today, July/August, 8-11

Mukherjee, T (1983) 'Collusion, Conflict or Constructive Antiracist Socialisation', Multicultural Teaching, 1, 2, 24-25

Mullard, C (1982) 'Multiracial Education in Britain: From Assimilation to Cultural Pluralism' in J Tierney (ed.) Race, Migration and Schooling, Holt, Rinehart and Winston, London, pp.120-133

Mullard, C (1984) Anti-Racist Education: The Three O's, National Association for Multiracial Education, Cardiff

Mullard, C, Bonnick, L and King, B (1983) Racial Policy and Practice: A Letter Survey, Race Relations Policy and Practice Research Unit, Institute of Education, London

National Association of Teachers in Further and Higher Education (1984) NATFHE Against Racism: A Draft NEC Statement, NATFHE, London

National Union of Teachers (1981) Combatting Racialism in Schools, NUT, London

Newsam, P (1984) 'One Flew Over the Cuckoo's Nest', The Times Educational Supplement, 23 March, 2

Parekh, B (1985) 'The Gifts of Diversity', The Times Educational Supplement, 29 March, 22-23

Parkinson, M (1982) 'Politics and Policy-Making in Education' in A Hartnett (ed.) The Social Sciences in Educational Studies, Heinemann Educational Books, London, pp.114-126

Passmore, B (1983) 'ILEA Guidelines on Racism Anger Teachers' Unions', The Times Educational Supplement, 7 October, 12

Patterson, S (1969) Immigration and Race Relations in Britain: 1960-1967, Institute of Race Relations/Oxford University Press, London

Popkewitz, T S (1984) Paradigm and Ideology in Educational Research, The Falmer Press, Sussex

Raffe, D. (1984) 'The Transition from School to Work and the Recession: Evidence from the Scottish School Leavers Survey 1977-1983', British Journal of Sociology of Education, 5, 3, 247-266

Reeves, F (1983) British Racial Discourse: A Study of British Political Discourse About Race and Race-Related Matters, Cambridge University Press, Cambridge

Reeves, F and Chevannes, M (1981) 'The Underachievement of Rampton', Multiracial Education, 10, 1, 35-42

Reeves, F and Chevannes, M (1983) 'The Ideological Construction of Black Underachievement', Multiracial Education, 12, 1, 22-41

Rex, J (1982) Race Relations in Sociological Theory (2nd edition), Routledge and Kegan Paul, London

Rex, J., Troyna, B and Naguib, M (1983) The Development of Multicultural Education Policy in Four Local Education Authority Areas, Unpublished Report Submitted to the Swann Committee of Inquiry into the Education of Children from Ethnic Minority Groups, Research Unit on Ethnic Relations, Aston University, Birmingham

Richardson, R (1983) Unemployment and the Inner City: A Study of School Leavers in London, Department of Environment, London

Richardson, R (1983) 'Worth the Paper it's Written On?' Issues in Race and Education, No. 40, 2-4

Roberts, K (1984) School-Leavers and their Prospects, Open University Press, Milton Keynes

Rose, E J B et al (1969) Colour and Citizenship, Institute of Race Relations/Oxford University Press, London

Royal Commission on Population (1949), HMSO, London

Salter, B and Tapper, T (1981) Education, Politics and the State, Grant McIntyre, London

Saunders, M (1982) 'Education For a New Community', New Community, 10, 1, 64-71

Scarman, The Rt. Hon. Lord (1981) The Brixton Disorders, 10-12 April 1981, (Cmnd. 8427), HMSO, London

Schools Council (1967) English for the Children of Immigrants (Working Paper No. 13), HMSO, London

Searle, C (1977) The World in a Classroom, Writers and Readers Publishing Company, London

Selbourne, D (1984) 'The Culture Clash in Bradford,' New Society, 26 April, 135-139

Select Committee on Race Relations and Immigration (1969) The Problems of Coloured School Leavers, HMSO, London

Select Committee on Race Relations and Immigration (1973) Education (Vol, 1), HMSO, London

Shallice, J (1984) 'Racism and Education' in ALTARF Challenging Racism, All London Teachers Against Racism and Fascism, London, pp. 3-14

Sharp, R (1984) 'Urban Education and the Current Crisis' in G Grace (ed.) Education and the City, Routledge and Kegan Paul, London, pp.60-93

Simon, B (1984) 'Breaking School Rules', Marxism Today, September, 19-25

Sitkoff, H (1981) The Struggle for Black Equality, 1954-1980, Hill and Wang, New York

Sivanandan, A (1981/2) 'From Resistance to Rebellion: Asian and Afro-Caribbean Struggles in Britain', Race and Class, 23, 2/3, 111-152

Sivanandan, A (1983) 'Challenging Racism: Strategies for the 1980s', Race and Class, 25, 2, 1-11

Sivanandan, A. (1985) 'RAT and the Degradation of the Black Struggle', Race and Class, 26, 4, 1-33

Sivanandan, N (1984) 'The Changing Face of Racism in London's Schools', Schooling and Culture, No. 14, 38-43

Solomos, J (1983) The Politics of Black Youth Unemployment, Working Papers on Ethnic Relations No. 20, Research Unit on Ethnic Relations, Aston University, Birmingham

Solomos, J (Forthcoming) 'Varieties of Marxist Conceptions of "Race", Class and the State: A Critical Analysis' in J Rex and D Mason (eds.), Theories of Race and Ethnic Relations, Cambridge, Cambridge University Press

Bibliography

Sowell, T (1981) Ethnic America, Basic Books, New York
Spears, A K (1978) 'Institutional Racism and The Education of Blacks', Anthropology and Education Quarterly, 9, 2, 127-136
St John, N (1975) School Desegregation: Outcomes for Children, John Wiley, New York
Stone, M (1981) The Education of the Black Child in Britain, Fontana, London
Straker-Welds, M (ed.), (1984) Education For a Multicultural Society: Case Studies in ILEA Schools, Bell and Hyman, London
Stubbs, P (1985) The Employment of Black Social Workers: From Ethnic Sensitivity to Antiracism?' Critical Social Policy, No. 12, 6-27
Taylor, B (1984-5) 'Multicultural Education in a "Monocultural" Region', New Community, 12, 1, 1-8
Tomlinson, S (1981a) 'Inexplicit Policies in Race and Education', Education Policy Bulletin, 9, 2, 149-166
Tomlinson, S (1981b) Educational Subnormality, Routledge and Kegan Paul, London
Townsend, H E R (1971) Immigrant Pupils in England: the LEA Response, NFER, Slough
Townsend, H E R and Brittan, E (1972) Organisation in Multiracial Schools, NFER, Slough
Troyna, B (1982) 'The Ideological and Policy Response to Black Pupils in British Schools' in A Hartnett (ed.) The Social Sciences in Educational Studies, Heinemann Educational Books, London, pp.127-143
Troyna, B (1983) 'Multiracial Education: Just Another Brick in the Wall?,' New Community, 10, 3, 424-428
Troyna, B (1984a) 'Fact or Artefact? The "Educational Underachievement" of Black Pupils', British Journal of Sociology of Education, 5, 2, 153-166
Troyna, B (1984b) 'Multicultural Education: Emancipation or Containment?' in L Barton and S Walker (eds.) Social Crisis and Educational Research, Croom Helm, Beckenham, pp.75-97
Troyna, B (1984c) '"Policy Entrepreneurs" and the Development of Multi-Ethnic Education Policies: A Reconstruction', Educational Management and Administration, 12, 3, 203-212
Troyna, B (1985a) 'The "Racialisation" of Contemporary Education Policy: Its Origins, Nature and Impact in a Period of Contraction' in G Walford (ed.), Schooling in Turmoil, Croom Helm, Beckenham, pp.38-58
Troyna, B (1985b) 'The Great Divide: Policies and Practice in Multicultural Education', British Journal of Sociology of Education, 6, 2, 209-224
Troyna, B and Ball, W (1983) 'Multicultural Education Policies: Are They Worth the Paper They're Written On?' The Times Educational Supplement, 9 December, 20
Troyna, B and Ball, W (1984) 'Multicultural Education Policy in Practice', The Runnymede Trust Bulletin, Race and Immigration, No. 166, 7-15

Troyna, B and Ball, W (1985a) 'Styles of LEA Policy Intervention in Multicultural/Antiracist Education', Educational Review, 37, 2, 165-173

Troyna, B and Ball, W (1985b) Views from the Chalk Face: School Responses to an LEA's Multicultural Education Policy Policy Papers on Ethnic Relations, University of Warwick, Coventry

Troyna, B and Smith D (eds.), (1983) Racism, School and the Labour Market, National Youth Bureau, Leicester

del Tufo, S et al, (1982) ' Inequality in a School System' in A Ohri, B Manning and P Curno (eds.) Community Work and Racism, Routledge and Kegan Paul, London, pp. 75-87

Van Den Berghe, P (1984) 'Race Perspective Two' in EE Cashmore (ed.) Dictionary of Race and Ethnic Relations, Routledge and Kegan Paul, London, pp. 216-218

Weintraub, A. (1972) Race and Local Politics in England: A Case Study of Willesden, Ph.D. Thesis, Columbia University, New York

Wellman, D (1977) Portraits of White Racism, Cambridge University Press, Cambridge

Whitty, G (1983) 'State Policy and School Examinations, 1976-1982' in J Ahier and M Flude (eds.) Contemporary Education Policy, Croom Helm, Beckenham, pp. 165-190

Willey, R (1984) Race, Equality and Schools, Methuen, London

Williams, J (1967) 'The Younger Generation' in J Rex and R Moore Race Community and Conflict, Institute of Race Relations/Oxford University Press, London, pp. 230-257

Williams, J (1981) 'Race and Schooling: Some Recent Contributions', British Journal of Sociology of Education, 2, 2, 221-227

Williams, J (forthcoming) 'Redefining Institutional Racism: Theoretical, Empirical and Political Issues', Ethnic and Racial Studies

Williams, J and Carter, B (1985) ' "Institutional Racism": New Orthodoxy, Old Ideas', Multiracial Education, 13, 1, 3-8

Willis, P (1977) Learning to Labour, Saxon House, Farnborough

Willis, P (1983) 'Cultural Production and Theories of Reproduction' in L Barton and S Walker (eds.) Race, Class and Education Croom Helm, Beckenham, pp.109-138

Wilson, A (1984) 'Educating Patrick', New Statesman, 25 May, 14

Young, K and Connelly, N (1981) Policy and Practice in the Multi-Racial City, Policy Studies Institute, London